DECODE and CONQUER

Answers to Product Management Interviews

LEWIS C. LIN

This book is dedicated to my parents, sister and wife. Thanks for supporting my passion for business and helping me push past my fears to embrace entrepreneurship.

Published by Impact Interview, 677 120th Ave NE, Suite 2A-241, Bellevue, WA 98105.

The author and publisher have made every effort to ensure the accuracy and completeness of information contained in this book. However, we assume no responsibility for errors, inaccuracies, omissions, or any inconsistency herein. Any slights of people, places, or organizations are intentional.

Corporations, organizations, and educational institutions: bulk quantity pricing is available. For information, contact lewis@impactinterview.com.

SECOND EDITION

Lin, Lewis C.
Decode & Conquer: Answers to Product Management Interviews / Lewis C. Lin.

Table of Contents

CHAPTER 14 CREATING VISION 177

CHAPTER 15 PASSING THE STRESS TEST 186

CHAPTER 16 WINNING THE BEHAVIORAL INTERVIEW 193

Introduction

Teaching is a passion of mine, and I'm thrilled to share my knowledge about product management interviews with this book. Over the last five years, I've helped job seekers get their dream jobs. During that period, I've taught my clients the fundamentals of product management, design, business, technology, and face-to-face communication.

Over the years, my clients have asked me for sample answers for case interview questions for the likes of Google, Amazon, Facebook, LinkedIn and Microsoft. To my clients, you've inspired me to write that book. I hope you enjoy it.

This book focuses on sample answers. On the Internet, there is no shortage of tips and frameworks on how to answer these questions. But actual answer responses — that's rare. That's what you'll get here.

This book also provides context without which you may not understand why a particular question would be asked or if your planned response is good or bad. I have provided some brief advice before each question type on how to approach a particular category of questions.

The product management case interview is tough. It combines interview questions that would otherwise for appear for positions in disparate disciplines, including project management, product design, software engineering, management consulting and marketing.

The best way to prepare is to practice. This book will help you develop responses with the help of sample answers. You won't be caught off guard with unexpected interview questions. You will be able to analyze differences between responses and determine what's best for you. When the big interview day comes, with your newfound awareness and knowledge, your responses will be convincing and penetrating.

The aim of the book is not to give you a script to read from during an interview, but to prepare you for whatever questions may come your way. By working with this book, your response will sound practiced, but not in the regurgitated way that interviewers can easily detect. In fact, the book will prepare you to answer unique employer-specific questions that aren't in this book.

This book will prepare you for an interview both by helping you with your content and your delivery. For the sake of simplicity, I refer to hypothetical candidates as "he" and hypothetical interviewers as "she."

There is no substitute for true, in-depth knowledge. That is the product manager's burden. You have to be an expert in so many different fields. Over time, if you haven't already, you should develop intellectual curiosity for all the product management disciplines – from design to business to technical. You'll find that interview responses will come more naturally.

In addition to the content of your answers, delivery is equally important. Good product management candidates give answers that are impactful, influential, engaging and precise. Many ineffective candidates ramble at the same cadence as dull corporate jargon. It's important to be crisp in your responses and avoid boring answers.

Good luck with your interviews. By challenging yourself and practicing, you won't need it!

November 2013

Chapter 1 Critiquing Design

Any good design critique includes a scorecard. It's an objective way to determine if a product passes or fails based on predetermined criteria.

Dieter Rams is a famous industrial designer who has deeply influenced Apple's design chief, Jony Ive. Rams has 10 design principles that governs his work. It serves as a good starting point to evaluate product or feature design.

Dieter Rams Ten Principles of Good Design

Good design is:

1. **Innovative**
2. **Makes a product useful**
3. Aesthetic
4. **Understandable**
5. Unobtrusive
6. **Honest**
7. Long-lasting
8. Thorough down to the last detail
9. Environmentally friendly
10. As little design as possible

Of his 10 design principles, I've bolded the best ones to cite: innovation, utility, ease of use and sense of honesty.

Approach any product design critique by:

- Revealing your design criteria. Cap it to three principles.
- Explaining how the product may or may not meet your criteria.
- Being specific, offering evidence, and contrasting with similar products.

Practice Questions

1. How do you like LinkedIn's endorse feature?
2. Tell me about a product you like and use frequently. Why do you like it?
3. Tell me about a product that was designed poorly.

Answers

How do you like LinkedIn's endorse feature?

CANDIDATE: When I evaluate whether or not I like a feature, I think about three design principles:

- Is it innovative?
- Is it useful?
- Is it honest?

I'll use those principles to evaluate LinkedIn's endorse feature.

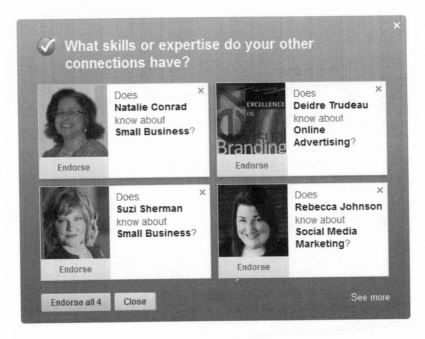

Since I don't recall the feature details, I will start by reviewing how the feature works. The endorse feature appears on different parts of the site.

On your profile page

There's a pop-up at the top of the page asking you to endorse skills of four people you know.

LinkedIn offers suggestions for endorsements. You can endorse each person individually, or you can easily endorse everyone by clicking a single button.

On someone else's profile page

Here we are at Matt's profile page. It focuses on suggestions for Matt alone, not four different people. There are a few suggestions — with the ability to add or subtract endorsement. Suggested endorsements could be added to Matt's profile with a single click of the yellow "Endorse" button, provided that Matt accepts them.

9	Product Management	▸
6	Social Media	▸
6	Business Strategy	▸
5	Product Requirements	▸
5	Product Planning	▸
3	Consumer Internet	▸
3	Business Planning	▸
3	Digital Media	▸
2	Strategic Consulting	▸
2	Go-to-market Strategy	▸

All endorsements appear at the bottom of a user's profile page. On the left, you'll see how many have endorsed a particular skill. On the right, you'll find photos for those who gave the endorsement.

	Pros	Cons
Innovative	Is a clever way to get more profile data	May not produce quality data
Useful	Adds more information about the individual. Identifies probable expertise areas	Has categories that don't include details or examples
Honest	Provides wisdom of the crowds	Lacks way to verify what is actually true

The feature is innovative though it has issues. I find it a clever way to get more profile data. It's an easy one-click process. And the endorsee will be compelled to return the favor to the endorser, creating a growing cycle of more endorsement data.

But the data quality is suspect. On the one hand, LinkedIn doesn't allow strangers to endorse one another. But still, who knows if the endorser is qualified to evaluate a person's expertise?

The feature meets my usefulness criteria. LinkedIn wants people to find the site valuable and worth spending time on. Users are more likely to spend time on it if there's more quality data to peruse. The data also has two additional benefits to LinkedIn. First, LinkedIn can create new products based on rich data. Second, for a competitor to lure the LinkedIn user, it would take a lot of time to recreate all the value that already exists on LinkedIn. The downside is that these endorsements don't include examples or details of a person's expertise. For example, if someone is endorsed as an expert in web design, I'd like to see a link to his or her design portfolio.

The third and final criteria for me, is this feature honest? I have mixed feelings about that. On the one hand, it leverages the wisdom of the crowds. On the other hand, there's a heavy sampling bias. Friends are more likely to endorse each other than people with other types, or no, relationships. Also, endorsed users feel compelled to return the favor, possibly voting up connections that shouldn't have been voted up in the first place.

Comments: The candidate does a good job stating his evaluation criteria and then thoughtfully evaluated the feature based on those criteria.

Walking through, either in writing or vocally, the way the feature works may seem unnecessary. However, most candidates overestimate their knowledge of a particular product. They assume they know how it works, only to be challenged by the interviewer later when the feature doesn't work that way. By methodically

walking through the product before critiquing it, the candidate takes the opportunity of being on the same page as the interviewer before moving forward.

Tell me about a product you like and use frequently. Why do you like it?

CANDIDATE: My favorite product is my iPhone. When I think about why it's my favorite, it comes down to three key design questions:

- How useful is it?
- How innovative is it?
- Is the product easy to use and understood?

In terms of utility, there's no other device that I use as much as my iPhone. It's a personal communication device that allows me to browse the web and listen to music. Excluding eating and breathing, it meets or helps meet most of my life needs including getting stuff done and connecting with friends and family.

It's a very innovative product. Before the iPhone, the BlackBerry dominated. BlackBerries were effective for emailing, but they were limited when browsing the web. And there were few apps. Remember checking sports scores on a WAP-enabled (wireless application protocol) ESPN site? It seems archaic compared with what we have now. We've come a long way, and the iPhone gets most of the credit for starting the revolution.

Finally, the product is easy to use and understand. There are few buttons — just the ones that are critical and obvious: on/off, ringer mute, and volume controls. Perhaps the only non-obvious button is the home button, but fortunately, that button is easy to figure out.

Navigation is simple. Just use your finger. And it fits cleanly with pre-existing mental models. You scroll through pictures as if you're flipping through a photo album.

To recap, I like the iPhone because it meets my three criteria for great products. It's useful, innovative and easy to understand.

Comments: The candidate answers the question honestly. He makes it easy for the interviewer to evaluate the response since the candidate specified criteria. The candidate also backed up his comments with evidence and compared the iPhone with peer products. The response could have been more memorable if the candidate chose a unique product.

Tell me about a product that was designed poorly.

CANDIDATE: When I think about a product that was designed poorly, I think of the Apple's hockey-puck mouse from the 1998 iMac. There are three reasons why:

First, it doesn't work well. The round shape made it hard to orient. Without looking at the mouse, you cannot tell if you are holding it right side up, upside down, sideways. The mouse could have used some tactile cues to help determine its orientation.

Second, the design was excessive. The blue accents on the left and right do not deliver additional function. It could be misconstrued for buttons.

Third, the round shape was unique but not useful. Holding the mouse was just awkward.

Comments: A solid response from the candidate. It's a unique product choice. Few candidates would mention this particular product. And at first glance, it's ironic that Apple, a product design leader, would be called out for bad design. There's a lot of thought and evidence included in this response, which lends the answer credibility and sincerity.

Chapter 2 Designing a Desktop Application

The product design questions are some of the most dreaded questions in the product management interview. Candidates tend to stumble in four areas when it comes to the product design interview.

Reasons Why Candidates Stumble

Starting. I can't tell you how many times I receive that "Oh, no!" deer in headlights look.

Rambling. The candidate doesn't have a clue how to answer. He tries to improvise a solution as he is talking. It's painful for the listener.

Ending the response. Candidates find it uncomfortable to stop, unsure if the interviewer is satisfied with his answer.

Focusing on the solution only. Giving a solution without the appropriate context begs the question, "Why?" The listener doesn't know who the intended customer is or what problem the product solves. And it's not clear why this is the best solution, relative to other possibilities.

I created the CIRCLES Method™ to answer any design question. Use it for questions on how you would design a new desktop, website, or mobile application. You can even use it to design new consumer products like a car, camera or can opener.

CIRCLES Method™ is a guideline on what makes a complete, thoughtful response any design question. It's a memory aid that prevents us from forgetting a step in the interview.

In case you forget, remember that designers love circles. Therefore the CIRCLES Method™ is perfect for design questions.

What is the CIRCLES Method™?

C omprehend the Situation

I dentify the Customer

R eport the Customer's Needs

C ut, Through Prioritization

L ist Solutions

E valuate Tradeoffs

S ummarize Your Recommendation

Comprehend the Situation

Not too long ago, I asked a candidate, "Pretend you are a Windows 8 product manager. How would you improve it?" I stopped her 45 seconds into her response. She rambled and used nonsense phrases like "Windows 8 deepens customer empowerment."

I asked her, "Have you used Windows 8?" She sheepishly replied, "Never. I use a MacBook Air."

Sigh. I don't want anyone performing open-heart surgery if he or she doesn't know what the heart looks like. If you don't know the product, speak up. It's not fair for you to discuss a product you don't know.

You're entitled to ask the interviewer clarifying questions. What can or should you ask the interviewer?

Here's a list:

- **What is it?**
- **Who is it for?**
- **Why do they need it?**
- When is it available?
- Where is it available?
- **How does it work?**

This list of basic questions is frequently called the "5 W's and H." However, the interviewer may not have patience for you to ask 101 questions about the product. To start the interview, you really just need answers for the four bolded questions: what is it, who is it for, why do they need it, and how does it work? So we'll call our version the "3 W's and H."

If the interviewer refuses to answer your clarifying questions, make an assumption based on what you know. Then, give the interviewer an opportunity to correct you, in the event he thinks differently about whom it is for or how the product works.

I also recommend that you pull up the website, mobile app or application. A visual improves communication. And who knows, since we live in the world of rapid experimentation, the website that you saw yesterday may have changed today. Or if you're talking about a product that the interviewer is working on, it's possible they use a beta version internally, which is completely different from what you use. It would be lethal if you and the interviewer were thinking of different things.

Identify the Customer

There's no magical device that does everything for everyone. But that hasn't stopped companies from trying to build all-in-one devices. As sexy as they sound, more often than not, all-in-ones usually aren't very good.

During the interview, you want to propose an amazing product, not a mediocre one. To do so, focus on a single customer segment or persona.

Start the second step of the CIRCLES Method™ by listing potential customer personas. Here are some examples:

- Food lovers
- Soccer moms
- College students
- Small business owners

Time is limited, so choose one persona to focus on. The interviewer may not be familiar with your chosen persona; help them comprehend whom you are talking about. A 2 x 2 matrix is a powerful way to visualize it.

Kat, the traveling reader	Behaviors
	• Goes on vacations with books • Travels four times a year • Carries four books per trip
Demographics	Needs & Goals
• 55 year old, single female • Lives in Hoquiam, Washington • Income: $70,000 USD	• Discover new books • Discuss books with others • Write a book one day

Photo credit: Joe Crawford

Report the Customer's Needs

The third step of the CIRCLES Method™ is reporting the customer's needs. You can call it user needs, user requirements, or use cases. In modern product development, the use case format is a popular way to capture user needs. A user story conveys what the end user wants to do in normal everyday language. It does not describe how the solution works. Here's the user story template:

As a <role>, I want <goal/desire> so that <benefit>.

Here are two examples based on our persona, Kat, our traveling reader:

Book discovery

As a traveling reader, I want to get recommendations so that I read books that are either well-written or are good examples of my favorite genres.

Write a book

As a traveling reader, I want to write 500 words a day so that I can publish my memoir.

User stories have become popular because they are concise, complete and casual. In a single sentence, we know the user, the user's needs and user's justification.

Cut, Through Prioritization

Looking at our "book discovery" and "write a book" use cases above, each one screams for completely different solutions. Step four of the CIRCLES Method™ is to cut, through prioritization.

The prioritization step mimics the real world development process. You'll have a big backlog of use cases, but you're limited by time, money, and labor. Which one do you do first?

In the interview, you don't have time to talk through all use cases. So you'll have to pick one. When you make your choice, it's an opportunity to showcase your ability to make prioritize, assess tradeoffs and make decisions.

User Story	Revenue	Customer Satisfaction	Ease of Implementation	Overall
Write a book	A	A	A	A
Book discovery	C	C	C	C

The prioritization matrix above is an example. It shows how a product manager can be thoughtful about choosing priorities.

Real world prioritization is not that different from the matrix above. That is, it's based on subjective criteria, weights and grades. Despite some flaws, I feel the matrix is effective. I'd rather have an imperfect process than no process at all. The matrix method forces the decision maker to think and articulate what's important. Is revenue more important? Or is customer satisfaction? Ultimately, the true arbiter of go versus no-go for a particular feature should be A/B testing.

If you're looking for an even more thoughtful and quantitative approach to prioritization, you could estimate the revenue impact and investment, measured in engineering effort. From there, you can calculate ROI-like metric, which I call revenue per point of effort.

User Story	Revenue impact	Story size	Revenue per point of effort	Priority
Write a book	$500,000	8	$62,500	1
Book discovery	$20,000	2	$10,000	2

Note: "Story size" is a metric to estimate the engineering effort necessary to complete a story.

List solutions

Step five of the CIRCLES Method™ is to list solutions. Most candidates freeze when they have a design problem without a solution on the tip of their tongue. Brainstorming frameworks can help overcome designer's block. Here are my three favorites:

Reversal method. Reversing the situation helps uncover new possibilities.

Example: Create a new car buying experience.

Need: Buyers don't have time to travel to the car dealership.

Solution based on reversal: Dealership should deliver test drives to the buyer's home.

Attribute method. List all the product attributes. Mix and match to get interesting new combinations.

Example: Design a new laundry hamper.

Material	Shape	Finish	Position
Wicker	Square	Natural	Sits on floor
Plastic	Cylindrical	Painted	On ceiling
Paper	Rectangle	Clear	On wall
Metal	Hexagonal	Luminous	Basement chute
Net material	Cube	Neon	On door

Solution based on attributes: I suggest we build a **rectangle, plastic** hamper with a **natural** finish that can be mounted **on the door**.

Why? Method. Challenge the status quo.

Example: Design a new coffee cup.

Start by challenging the status quo: Why should coffee cups have handles? Cups are too hot to hold directly.

Solution based on Why? Method: Create a coffee mug with an insulation layer.

I have two more tips when listing potential product solutions.

Tip #1: Think big

Your typical candidate usually list solutions that fall into one of two categories:

- *Me too ideas.* For example, "As the Google+ product manager, I would create a new feature that's similar to Facebook's groups feature." Yawn.
- *Integration ideas.* For instance, "As the Google product manager, I would integrate YouTube with Android." Yawn.

As part of the interview, most employers are evaluating your creativity or product vision. They're looking for product managers that can see future trends, both in technology and customer behavior. They expect those product managers to plot and execute a plan that exploits that trend, for the company's benefit.

To help spur your thinking, consider the following big bets from the tech industry leaders:

- In 2008, Google made a $4.6 billion bid for wireless spectrum. How did Google have the gravitas to make a multi-billion dollar bid when Google had no experience as a wireless operator? Google had guts. In the end, it was one of the biggest bluffs in business history. Google didn't win the bid, but they didn't want to. They got the FCC to adopt open access rules that would force the winner to allow any Google device or application to connect to this new spectrum. That privilege was worth billions to Google. And they got it for free.

- That same year, Facebook launched Facebook Connect. Facebook encouraged developers to use Facebook as their sign-in service. Facebook positioned the feature as trustworthy and easy-to-use. Developers could now devote time that would have gone into building proprietary sign-up and sign-on systems for something else. And web and mobile applications would have access to a user's valuable Facebook data. But Facebook had the biggest win. Facebook Connect allowed Facebook to track user behavior around the web. They knew which websites a user visited and what mobile apps they used. They could use this data to build better products, and more importantly, deliver more targeted ads. Facebook makes billions from advertising. Better ad targeting can easily lead to a 500 percent increase in revenue.

Tip #2: Have at least three ideas

Great innovators know that your first idea is rarely the best. Why? Innovation is an iterative process. As you learn more about customer needs and competitive products, your proposed solutions will be more precise and focused. You'll avoid ideas that have failed in the marketplace.

At the interview, brainstorm at least three ideas. It's hard but it'll be worth it. You'll find that idea number 2 or 3 will usually be the best of the bunch.

Also, it will help you from being defensive during the interview. The interviewer will critique your idea. If you have only one idea, you'll take it personally. If you have multiple ideas, you'll be more comfortable because you'll have other solutions to prove your self-worth.

Evaluate Tradeoffs

The sixth step of the CIRCLES Method™ is to evaluate tradeoffs. The first part is optional: define your tradeoff criteria. Criteria could include customer satisfaction, implementation difficulty, and revenue potential. It's not necessary, but it'll keep your response organized and easier to follow.

The next part is analyzing the solution. A pro and cons list is a good way to do this.

By evaluating tradeoffs of each solution, you come across as thoughtful and analytical. You'll also be perceived as objective.

You'll also protect yourself from being defensive. If you've taken the initiative to critique your own solutions, the interviewer has fewer things to criticize. You'll also mentally prepare yourself for criticism by critiquing yourself.

Summarize Your Recommendation

The seventh step of the CIRCLES Method™ is to summarize your recommendation. This is an optional step; sometimes the interviewer is satisfied with a brainstorm and the pro and con analysis.

But others want to test your communication and decision making skills. That is, can you present a short 20 to 30 second summary of your product proposal? And can you make the hard decision to suggest just one solution?

Summarize with this three-step approach:

1. Tell the interviewer which product or feature you'd recommend.
2. Recap on what it is and why it's beneficial to the user and/or company.
3. Explain why you preferred this solution vs. others.

Tip on using the CIRCLES Method™

My clients often struggle with design questions because they're uncomfortable exploring customers and needs without a solution. If that's the case, it's okay to have a solution in mind and lead your CIRCLES Method™ discussion toward it.

It's important for you to exude confidence during the design discussion, and if this is what makes you feel better, fantastic. I also find that having a solution in mind can help constrain the realm of potential personas, needs, and solutions, which can improve the quality of your responses.

Ultimately, I would love for you to embrace the great unknown and enjoy a design problem without having a solution in mind.

Practice Question

1. How would you improve Microsoft PowerPoint?

Answer

How would you improve Microsoft PowerPoint?

CANDIDATE: Here's how I would improve Microsoft PowerPoint.

Candidate writes the following on whiteboard.

- *Goals & constraints*
- *User & use cases*
- *Prioritize use cases*
- *Brainstorm solutions*

First, I'd make sure that I understand our goals & constraints; then, I'd explore the user and use cases; and lastly, I'd prioritize the use cases and focus on brainstorming solutions for the most urgent use case.

INTERVIEWER: Sounds good.

Candidate writes the following on whiteboard.

- *Revenue*
- *Engagement*

CANDIDATE: We can consider different goals, such as increasing revenue and engagement. I have revenue in mind, but is there another goal that you prefer to discuss?

INTERVIEWER: I'd like you to focus on revenue.

CANDIDATE: Okay, let's focus on revenue. It is fair to assume that we will increase revenue by selling an add-on to Microsoft PowerPoint?

INTERVIEWER: Sure, this new product is going to be an add-on product.

CANDIDATE: There are different personas we can consider. Just rattling a few off the top of my head…

Candidate draws the following on the whiteboard.

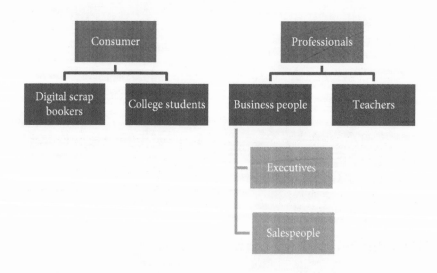

CANDIDATE: Which persona would you like to focus on?

INTERVIEWER: Salespeople.

CANDIDATE: Based on my understanding, salespeople use PowerPoint primarily for customer presentations. Their desire is to win a business deal. When working on PowerPoint, here are the use cases that come to mind:

1. Need to figure out what to say
2. Need to figure out how to say it
3. Need to determine how to visually communicate that message

Of these different use cases, you can't solve the latter two without solving the first one. So I feel the first one is most important. If you approve, I'll brainstorm solutions for that use case.

INTERVIEWER: Go ahead.

CANDIDATE: In response to the need to figure out what to say, there are a couple ideas that come to mind:

- **Pitch Builder** that will provide a guided process to build a pitch, using proven, compelling templates. There are salespeople who have the motivation to put together a good story, as long they can be guided through it. This is a concept first shared in *Switch* by Chip and Dan Heath.
- **Inspiration Gallery** that will set up a gallery where individuals can submit their favorite, proven sales pitches. Contributors establish their sales expertise and reputation by sharing proven pitches, and users learn from others' best practices.
- **Expert Marketplace** will deliver a marketplace where users can find experts that can provide pitch building advice

INTERVIEWER: What's your recommendation?

CANDIDATE: Of all the ideas, I prefer Pitch Builder. I believe in the power of templates, and a step-by-step story-building wizard is how professional presenters build effective PowerPoint presentations.

Comments: The candidate does a solid job exploring goals, customer needs and suggests a solution that solves a real problem.

Chapter 3 Designing a Webpage or Website

Apply the same CIRCLES Method™ when asked to design a webpage or website.

Tip: Interview Visually

A product manager's job is to effectively communicate their ideas and pictures often express ideas better than words.

During the product management interview, take this to heart. When critiquing a website or product, have visuals accessible and ready for display. When introducing an idea, be prepared to walk up to the whiteboard and sketch out wireframes. Standing up with a pen in hand, and leading an audience, even an audience of one, through a design critique or proposal feels authoritative. Hiring managers want product management candidates that radiate leadership.

If you want to really impress the interviewer, redesign a webpage at home, using your favorite mockup tool whether it's Balsamiq, Adobe Photoshop, or Microsoft PowerPoint. Bring copies of your visuals to the interview, and subtly introduce your redesign at the beginning of the interview. You can say, "When I was preparing for the interview, I couldn't help but redesign your profile page. (Share your visuals.) We can talk about my redesign during the interview, if you'd like."

This tactic will absolutely melt hearts. It stands out. Few candidates take the initiative and effort to do this. Others don't do this because they're afraid. They either find this tactic unconventional or they're afraid to commit their design ideas to paper.

Let's think about it. There's a strong likelihood they'll ask you a design question at the interview. Would you rather come up with a half-baked solution at the interview? Or would you rather spend a Sunday thinking through several variations and polishing up something presentable on Adobe Photoshop?

To move onto the next round or to get a job offer, it's simply about two things: credibility and likeability. Visually sharing your ideas portrays confidence in your design skills.

Practice Questions

1. How will you improve LinkedIn's home page?
2. How would you improve LinkedIn's signup process?
3. How would you improve image search?
4. How would you improve restaurant search?
5. How would you improve Google Maps?
6. You are the product manager for Google+. What killer feature would you build?
7. How would you improve Google's Chrome browser?

Answers

How will you improve LinkedIn's home page?

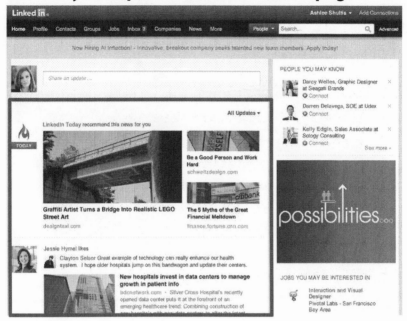

CANDIDATE: Before I make suggestions, I want to review the webpage, make sure I understand all the features, and ask clarifying questions.

INTERVIEWER: Sure.

CANDIDATE: My first thought: who is this page for? It's targeted to the LinkedIn user. The second thought: what does it do?

Candidate points to the big red box, above

CANDIDATE: I believe the primary goal is to show an evolving news feed. Here we see general news, but we could also get updates on our social network — whether people got a new job, connected to other people or received new skill endorsements.

Candidate points to the top two red sections, above

CANDIDATE: The secondary goal is to allow the user to post updates and discover new connections.

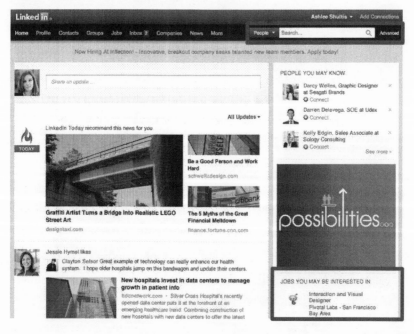

Candidate points to the two red sections on the right hand side, above

CANDIDATE: The third goal is to search for people and identify new jobs.

Just to summarize, there are four things that one could do on this page:

1.   Read updates for the work world, including general news and social updates.

2.   Write updates.

3.   Discover new contacts.

4.   Identify new job opportunities.

Now that I'm more familiar with the home page, let's dive into the question. My first thought: what's the purpose of the redesign? I'm specifically thinking of business objectives such as increasing ad revenue, LinkedIn connections, or 30-day actives. I define 30-day actives as the number of LinkedIn users that have visited the site in the last 30-days.

I'd propose looking at increasing 30-day actives, but I'm open to other suggestions too.

INTERVIEWER: No. Let's focus on engagement.

CANDIDATE: Next, I want to have a customer in mind for the redesign. Here are four personas that come to my mind:

- *The newsreader.* Officially, this persona is discovering new content to help them with their job. Unofficially, they are wasting time or procrastinating.
- *The social networker.* This person is keeping tabs on business relationships, hoping that it'll help him climb up the career ladder.

- *The job seeker.* Some job seekers will be employed. Others will be unemployed, but looking for better opportunities.
- *The salesperson.* Salespeople love LinkedIn because it is a treasure trove of contact information, interests, and needs. It's a great way to find new opportunities.

INTERVIEWER: Okay, we're short on time. Which persona do you want to focus on?

CANDIDATE: I'd like to focus on the salesperson.

INTERVIEWER: Go on.

CANDIDATE: What are the top use cases for salespeople? Here are the first three I thought of:

1. They're looking for new customer opportunities.
2. They want to strengthen relationships with existing customers. Most salespeople strengthen relationships by offering value: solving customer problems, providing information that moves their clients' business forward and yes, even providing perks like tickets to the customer's favorite sports team.
3. They want to get inspired. Selling products is tough. They get rejected all the time. Inspirational stories and words of encouragement help them soldier on.

In my opinion, the most important use case is finding new customer opportunities.

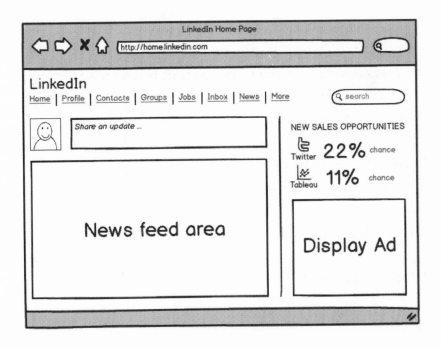

So let me share with you a mockup of what I envision.

Candidate points and walks through parts of the diagram

CANDIDATE: It's your standard LinkedIn newsfeed: logo, navigation, search box, news feed area, and display ad. Here's what's different: the "new sales opportunities" section in the upper right.

As the title describes, this feature proactively identifies new sales opportunities for the customer. For example, there are two new opportunities for Twitter and Tableau Software, a company that helps users display data publicly in attractive ways. Sales opportunities with Twitter and Tableau have a 22 percent and 11 percent chance to close, respectively. These predictions come from our algorithm, which analyzes sales opportunities based on a news event, similarity with existing customers, and the number of close connections to that company.

Clicking on "new sales opportunities," you'll see the next page, the "sales opportunity dashboard."

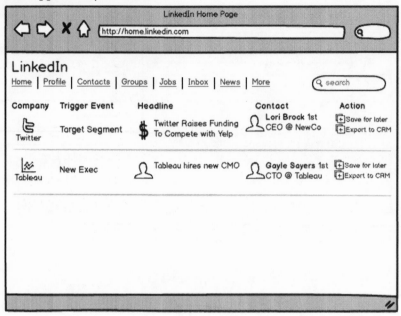

The candidate points to the next page, the sales opportunity dashboard.

CANDIDATE: On the sales opportunity dashboard, the sales person can get more details including:

- *Trigger event.* For the Twitter sales opportunity, the dashboard indicates that it's in the same "target segment" as one of our existing customers. Competitive companies usually have similar needs. They're also easier to close because of the powerful sales intro, "I'm calling because one of your competitors uses our software…"
- *Headline.* This is the news that triggered the event.
- *Contact.* Identifies a potential contact person, with the ability to click to see their LinkedIn profile.

- *Action.* User can bookmark a sales opportunity and export to their customer relationship management (CRM) software. As a future addition, perhaps LinkedIn can become the forum through which contact is made. For instance, there could be cold call email templates, progress tracking, automatic follow-up and reporting.

Comments: The candidate does a good job empathizing with the customer and exploring their needs. The focused choice of the salesperson persona helpfully constrained his creativity to a very specific use case, identifying new customer opportunities. The UI mockups demonstrate the candidate's ability to visually communicate a design.

How would you improve LinkedIn's signup process?

CANDIDATE: There are many pages in LinkedIn's signup flow. To make it manageable, I'm just going to go through one page at a time and discuss the pros, cons, and recommendations for each page.

INTERVIEWER: Sounds good.

Be great at what you do.

Get started – it's free.
Registration takes less than 2 minutes.

First name

Last name

Email address

Password 6 or more characters

Join now — By joining LinkedIn, you agree to LinkedIn's User Agreement, Privacy Policy and Cookie Policy.

"LinkedIn connects me to opportunities and talent in my area."
Mae O'Malley – Founding Attorney at Paragon Legal

CANDIDATE: Here's what I like the page. The testimonial validates the service, and the picture makes the service feel friendly. There's a single call-to-action, "Join now," with a simple registration process.

The one thing I hate about this page is the headline. The phrase "Be great at what you do" does not tell me what I'm signing up for. I'd recommend that we A/B test better headlines, especially ones that describe what the product does.

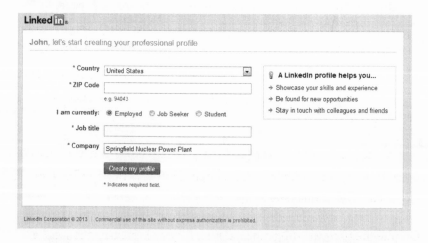

The copy on this page is much clearer than the previous page. The headline tells you that you're going to create a professional profile.

44

The radio buttons in the middle create a demarcation between the first two fields and the last two fields. I prefer if they had the Job title and Company fields on top vs. Country and ZIP Code. It seems like a more natural progression to the user.

I don't like that there's no indicator on how many steps are left. Lastly, "e.g. 94043" is visually awkward. I'd prefer if "94043" the default text in that field, just like "Springfield Nuclear Power Plant" is the default text.

Here the page copy regresses. "Grow your network on LinkedIn" is an ambiguous headline. Additionally, the page doesn't explain why it needs my email address and password.

From personal experience using LinkedIn, I do know that LinkedIn wants to help me add people to my network. One way they grow it is by importing contacts from my email application, checking whether they're already on LinkedIn and suggesting connections.

I would recommend testing explanatory text such as, "We make it easy to find colleagues on LinkedIn. Enter your email address and password, and we'll check if they're already on the site."

Despite the poor wording, it is a clever, easy and fast tactic to grow a new user's network. I bet that users with more connections perceive LinkedIn to be more valuable and use the site more.

As a minor aside, it is good to see that the progress bar is now present.

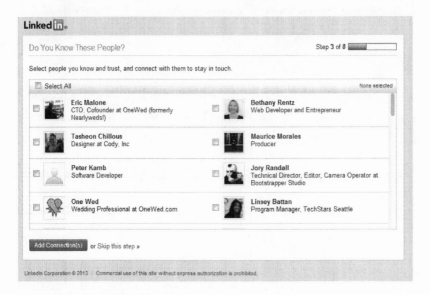

On this screen, LinkedIn suggests people to add to my network. That's helpful, but creepy.

How does LinkedIn (correctly) know that these people are related to me? As a user, the connection isn't quite clear. I've only submitted basic registration information: title name, country and zip code. How could it deduce that these people work with me, given that none of us work at the same company?

My guess is that they deduced these people based on the fact that all of us log into the service using the same IP address. That makes sense, since we all work in the same co-working space.

Still, I'm worried. How does LinkedIn know that these people are associated with me?

I would recommend that LinkedIn offer a link that explains how they generated these suggestions.

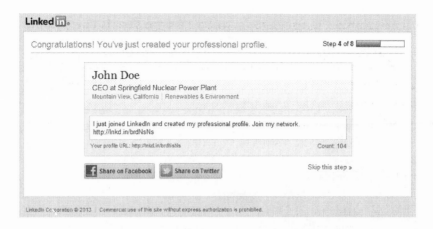

This screen is solid. I see a glimpse of what my LinkedIn profile would look like.

However, it asks me to share a message to my Facebook and Twitter networks. Why do they want me to share? I'd recommend that LinkedIn be clearer about why doing so would benefit me.

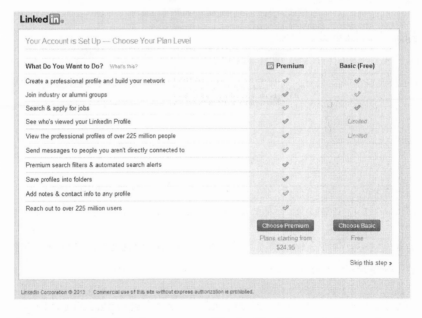

This is a nice, detailed description of LinkedIn. It's much better than the front page with its headline: "Be better at what you do."

Visually, the tabular comparison makes it easy to see what I get and don't get in the premium and free accounts.

However, the upsell feels premature. I just signed up for the service. How do I know if the free service is insufficient? The pricing is greyed out, which could be perceived as underhanded.

The final page I'll cover in my analysis is the profile page. I like how the blue box calls my attention. It's aligned with LinkedIn's desire to get me to add more data. The progress bar on the right shows how many more actions I need to complete. The checklist tells me how much further I need to go. I like how as I add information, my profile automatically updates. For example, when I added my picture, it automatically replaced the stock silhouette image with my picture.

The "finish later" option is a nice touch — just in case I'm fatigued from filling out forms.

Comments: Candidate does a solid job of critiquing what's working and not working on the page. However, compared to other candidates, this person did not offer as many suggestions on how to redesign the layout of the page. Most of the recommendations relate to the copy or the top-level objectives of the page.

How would you improve image search?

CANDIDATE: Before I begin, is the goal of improving image search is to improve usage and satisfaction of the product?

INTERVIEWER: Yes.

CANDIDATE: Are there any metrics or timeframes that I need to keep in mind?

INTERVIEWER: No.

CANDIDATE: Alright, when I think of image search, the first theme I think about is identification. I can think of a lot of personas who can benefit from image search including:

- Shoppers who might buy products they see at a friend's house.
- Artists who need to identify a particular font or color they see.
- Architect who need help classifying a building style.
- Consignment store owners who need to determine the value of secondhand goods.

The persona that intrigues me the most is the secondhand goods seller. I watch a lot of Pawn Stars, a reality TV show based on a Las Vegas pawnshop. I've also thought about starting a business in the consignment area.

INTERVIEWER: Okay, continue.

CANDIDATE: The two most critical activities in a pawnshop business are buying and selling products. Buying products that are fake, have low demand or cost too much are the main reasons why pawnshops fail.

I propose that we build a new image search feature that meets the need of the pawnshop owner. Here are top three use cases I have in mind:

1. *Identification.* By taking a picture of an object, the image search engine would quickly and probabilistically identify what the item is. For example, if it were a watch, it would determine so through the shape, color, features, and brand. It would narrow the universe of potential watches from tens of thousands to possibly 20-30 watches. This would help pawn shop owners save time and minimize errors when identifying products.

2. *Authentication.* Customers often try to pass off fake goods as the real thing, which hurts the pawnshop. Our image search engine can help with the authentication process. One idea is to offer a comprehensive feature checklist when evaluating a new purchase. For example, all Chanel bags have authenticity cards and quilting that always lines up. Another idea is to have an authenticity lookup, especially for manufacturers that assign unique serial numbers to products. Lastly, we could create a marketplace where pawnshop owners can get a crowd-sourced appraisal through Google's Hangout video conferencing technology.

3. *Valuation.* Once a product is identified, I propose that Google partner with eBay to get data on secondhand purchases. From there, Google can propose valuation ranges for a particular

product, based on an assessment of the product's condition. The ranges will be helpful in determining purchase price minimums and sell price maximums. For example, if a particular Chanel handbag has never sold for less than $300 on the used market, the pawn storeowner can buy that handbag with confidence for a $150 price.

Comments: Candidate brainstorms several good personas for image search. His focus on a single persona has come up with some innovative, albeit niche, applications for image search.

How would you improve restaurant search?

CANDIDATE: Before we begin, I have a few clarifying questions. When you say "restaurant search," I assume you're referring to finding restaurants in the Google search engine. This is specifically about recommendations, not necessarily finding a specific restaurant, right?

INTERVIEWER: Correct.

CANDIDATE: Before we start our discussion, I want to make sure I understand our objectives. I imagine we're looking to improve customer satisfaction around restaurant recommendations. We're not considering other goals, such as increasing revenue, page views, and any other goals?

INTERVIEWER: Bingo. We're focusing on user experience.

CANDIDATE: Perfect, give me a minute to collect my thoughts.

I see several potential target users. Here are a few that come to mind: first, there are out-of-town travelers who want to book restaurant reservations weeks in advance. Second, there's a person who wants restaurant recommendations for a group dinner. Third, there are working couples too tired to cook and needing a quick bite.

We don't have time to focus on all the personas; is there a specific one you'd like me to focus on?

INTERVIEWER: Yes, I'd like you to focus on couples.

CANDIDATE: Okay, we'll focus on working couples and talk about them in more detail. For working couples, it's usually a spur-of-the-moment decision. If they weren't so tired, they would have cooked at home and might have been cost-conscious with their food choices. The working couples we focus on are young professionals, so food quality is important to them. They wouldn't settle for McDonald's. They would want food that would be as tasty as what they would have cooked at home. They're busy and tired, so they want something close to home.

To summarize, their criteria in this scenario is:

- Quality.
- Time to eat.
- Price.

Let's prioritize our feature requests with the matrix below.

User Story	Customer Wow	Reasonable Alternatives	Implementation Difficulty	Overall
Quality indicator	Not impressed	Yes	Low	Lower priority
Time-to-eat indicator	Impressed	No	Med	Top priority
Price indicator	Not impressed	Yes	Low	Lower priority

INTERVIEWER: I like your prioritization matrix. Why don't you tell me how you would implement a time-to-eat indicator?

CANDIDATE: For the time-to-eat indicator, let's brainstorm some alternatives. Time to eat is dependent on three factors:

1. **Agreement**. In what amount of time could the two settle on where to eat?
2. **Travel**. How long does it take to travel to the restaurant?
3. **Food wait**. How long does the food to arrive after showing up at the restaurant?

Travel time information is available on Google Maps. Partner agreement can be factored in, too. Food wait seems to be hardest to implement and also intellectually interesting, so let's talk about that.

There are few ways we can estimate food wait times:

- Have a restaurant provide estimates.
- Have restaurant-goers provide estimates.
- Have a third-party information source provide wait times.

There could be a conflict of interest if restaurants provide food wait times, and as far as I know, there are no third-party information sources that provide wait time data.

There are several ways restaurant-goers can help us estimate wait times:

a. They could self-report via a survey or an extra field on a restaurant review. Self-reporting, though helpful, may not be accurate.
b. They can log the start and end times of their meal. This is better, but we would have to make an assumption on when the first appetizer or entrée arrived.
c. Lastly, restaurant-goers could check-in on the mobile app when they get to the restaurant and then take a picture of the first dish they receive.

INTERVIEWER: Which one would you recommend?

CANDIDATE: Of all the suggestions here, the last option is my favorite. It gives accurate data about how long it takes for a meal to arrive and the process of checking in and taking photos of food is a familiar process to food lovers, such as the Yelp mobile crowd.

Comments: Candidate distinguishes herself from other candidates by prioritizing the use cases. The time-to-eat feature is unique and likely to distinguish itself from competitors, especially for the "busy working couple" persona that the candidate identified.

How would you improve Google Maps?

CANDIDATE: Here's how I'd think about improving Google Maps. First, I'd understand our goals & constraints. Then, I'd explore the user and their use cases. I'd then prioritize the use cases and focus on brainstorming solutions for the most urgent use case.

We can consider different goals such as increasing revenue, new user acquisition, engagement and virality. I have engagement in mind, but is there another goal you prefer?

INTERVIEWER: Let's go forward with an engagement goal.

CANDIDATE: For users, there are a lot of audiences we can target: college students, young professionals, busy moms and retirees. I'd like to focus on brick-and-mortar shoppers. Is that okay with you?

INTERVIEWER: Sure.

CANDIDATE: For a shopper, one of the most frustrating things is when you can't find what you need. Warehouse stores, such as Home Depot, Costco and IKEA, are examples where this is a problem. You can imagine that there's a dollar cost to this frustration. Just imagine the time away from the job site, means billable hours lost.

There are a couple use cases we need to keep in mind. First, the user should be able to specify what product they're looking for. Second, they should confirm that it is the right product. Third, they should receive a detailed map location, including directions and shelf location. Lastly, it should indicate the number of units available.

Let's brainstorm solutions on how this might work. In the interest of time, let's just pick one area to focus on. Normally, we'd consider business value, customer impact and tech difficulty when prioritizing. In this case, let's just pick the most unique use case: the shelf locator.

INTERVIEWER: Okay.

CANDIDATE: The reason shelf locators are interesting is that a big box warehouse store – the aisles are several feet high and a mile deep – which makes this a big problem.

I have a few solutions in mind for a shelf locator feature. First idea is a picture that shows where a product is located. The picture will include surrounding products, to help the person locate it more easily, with the specific product highlighted in red.

The pro is that visual context helps to find things. The con is that it's not precise; the product could still be anywhere in the aisle. Also, it will be labor intensive to get all the pictures.

Second, we can label each product area. E.g. "Aisle 6, Section 2, Shelf 4." This is precise and easy-to-find. It does put a big burden on the storeowner to geo-label each product area.

The third idea is to tag each product with RFID chips. RFID chips emit a radio frequency to allow electronic devices to identify and track particular products. While RFID chips aren't cost prohibitive, not all shoppers have RFID readers on their phones. Attaching RFID chips to each product would require some tooling overhead.

I'm attracted to the RFID idea because it's cool, though honestly isn't the most pragmatic. In this case, the most pragmatic solution with respect to time, ease and cost of implementation is to simply label each product area.

Comments: It's a unique and thoughtful discussion on how to solve the "I can't find my product" problem. While the discussion is thoughtful, the choice of the shelf locator use case seemed a bit haphazard. The candidate did justify later it's a big problem, but the perception of his arbitrary decision-making had already solidified in the interviewer's mind.

You are the product manager for Google+. What killer feature would you build?

CANDIDATE: Great, let me first lay out how I'd like to tackle the problem and then we'll do a deep dive.

The candidate writes the following on the whiteboard:

- *Goals*
- *Constraints*
- *Personas*
- *Solutions*

CANDIDATE: I'd like to first understand what we are trying to achieve with product improvement. Then, I'd like to figure out the constraints in relation to building the product. Next, I'd like to probe into the customer types and their needs. Lastly, I'd like to discuss potential solutions.

INTERVIEWER: Sounds like a good plan.

CANDIDATE: Before I dive in, I'd like to make sure I have the same understanding of Google+ as you do. I understand that Google+ is a social network, where users can share information such as text, links, photos, and videos with other users. Google+ also includes the Google Hangout feature, allowing up to ten people to videoconference at once.

The second largest network after Facebook, Google+ has a reputation suggesting nothing much is happening there. Time spent on a social network is very much like time spent at a nightclub: The social network's popularity is based on who is there and what they do.

Is there anything that I'm missing?

INTERVIEWER: Nope, you've got the basic gist.

CANDIDATE: Our goal is to drive traffic to Google+.

INTERVIEWER: What does that mean? The word "traffic" is vague.

CANDIDATE: When I say "traffic," I mean user engagement. There are different ways to look at user engagement on Google+.

The candidate writes:

- *Number of sessions*
- *Session length*
- *Daily active*
- *Weekly actives*
- *Monthly actives*

CANDIDATE: I want to focus on increasing number of sessions per user.

INTERVIEWER: Okay, you want to increase the number of sessions per user. How much would you like to increase it and in what timeframe?

CANDIDATE: Let's shoot for a 10 percent increase in a one-year time frame.

INTERVIEWER: That hardly sounds like a killer feature to me. Let's aim for 30 percent growth in 3 months.

CANDIDATE: Okay, we'll go with that new number and explore customers.

INTERVIEWER: Thanks.

Candidate writes the following:

- *Primary persona: interacts with friends*
- *Secondary: occasionally messages friends online*
- *Negative: users who aren't social media regulars*

CANDIDATE: There are three personas we can consider. The primary persona is someone who interacts with friends a lot online, whether it's through instant message, SMS, or social networks. This person is our primary focus when building the new product.

The secondary persona is someone who doesn't spend a lot of time with friends online. If our new product meets this person's needs, perfect. If not, it's okay. We knew that this person would require some convincing.

The negative persona, or the person we won't focus on for the new product, is someone who isn't a social media regular.

INTERVIEWER: These personas are simplistic. You're basically just classifying users into heavy, normal, and low usage.

CANDIDATE: I want to build a product that has mass appeal, so I decided to classify them by social media usage versus demographic or psychographic dimensions.

INTERVIEWER: I'm not sold, but continue on.

CANDIDATE: Here are my three ideas for our primary persona:

Candidate writes the following:

- *Integrate Google Groups with Google+*
- *Integrate Blogger with Google+*
- *Share your most recently watched YouTube videos on Google+*

CANDIDATE: The first idea is for integration. Google+ doesn't offer good group functionality today. It's not like Facebook. There should be an easy way to join relevant groups and get updates.

Secondly, lots of people have Blogger websites, but Blogger is not integrated well into Google+. New blog posts should automatically be announced on Google+.

Lastly, a lot of Google users are watching YouTube videos. Google+ should integrate a YouTube users' viewing behavior into their Google+ feed.

INTERVIEWER: What you're suggesting is hardly groundbreaking. Most of your ideas are simple integration suggestions. In fact, we have a feature that addresses your second point.

CANDIDATE: This is the best way to leverage Google's various website assets and add more updates through the Google+ system.

INTERVIEWER: Fine. Out of all the ideas, which one do you think would have the biggest impact?

CANDIDATE: Integrating recently watched YouTube videos has the most potential. Over 1 billion unique visitors visit YouTube every month, creating a massive opportunity to put more content into a user's feed.

INTERVIEWER: Thank you.

Comments: The response was all over the place. The candidate makes a good attempt at demonstrating a logical problem-solving framework; however, the application of the framework is fairly mechanical, as demonstrated with the primary, secondary, and negative personas.

The candidate misses critical sections, including constraints and use cases. Goals and personas offer limited, useless insight. Solutions to the problem are unimpressive, especially considering the 30 percent growth target. The candidate also fails to clearly connect how his proposed solution will meet the 30 percent goal.

How would you improve Google's Chrome browser?

CANDIDATE: I'm assuming our improvement goal is to increase engagement, right?

INTERVIEWER: Yes.

CANDIDATE: There's a broad spectrum of Chrome users, but I'd like to focus on a specific customer persona: the developer. It's a group that identify closely with, and I feel their needs aren't being adequately met.

INTERVIEWER: Ok, tell me more about the developer.

CANDIDATE: More specifically, web developers. They have difficulty when it comes to testing and releasing new web sites and applications. Just from the top of my head, here are some use cases:

- Why aren't my webpages being indexed by Google properly?
- How can I identify miscoded or sub-optimally coded HTML & JavaScript pages?
- How can I quickly switch between my developer environment and the deployed environment without looking at the host file?
- How can I test my website from different locations around the world?
- How do I easily debug Flash elements on my webpage?

Since we don't have a lot of time, I'll just focus on what I think is a pressing issue for many web developers: why aren't my webpages being indexed by Google properly?

When it comes to Google indexing, there are three areas of concern:

1. Is it being indexed by Google?
2. Is it Google snippet displaying correctly?
3. Is it appearing high enough on the web page?

A page might not be indexed by Google if it's inaccessible. The server may be down (e.g. 404 error), robots.txt file explicitly blocks Google from accessing it, or there are DNS errors.

The Google snippet may not display correctly because the title and description tags may not have been edited correctly.

Lastly, web pages may not be appearing high enough because Google deems the pages to have a sub-par experience including:

- Number of domains linking to a page
- Number of Google +1's

- Page load time

I can think of three different ways to resolve the issue:

1. Create a toolbar that shows relevant debugging information.
2. Create a website that shows relevant information.
3. Provide a reporting service that provides the relevant info.

Of the three options, I like the first one the best. Developers would like to get the information inline, without getting yet another report or a website.

Comments: The candidate focused on a compelling persona: the developer. There's some interesting complexity here; however, we get the sense that he doesn't go deep enough. For instance, with the toolbar idea, it would have helped if he sketched a wireframe to give the interviewer an idea of what he had in mind.

Chapter 4 Designing a Mobile App

Apply the same CIRCLES Method™ when asked to design a mobile app.

Tip: Memorize Design Best Practices

Wire framing is not easy, especially if it's not something you do eight hours a day. How does one get inspiration for common design elements?

Full-time designers struggle with this too. One way to get inspiration is to look at competing sites. Another way is to reference a design pattern library. Design patterns are documented solutions to common problems. For instance, there are common user interface solutions for news feeds, listing pages, and navigation menus.

Before your interview, take a moment to review popular design patterns. There's no need to design news feeds from scratch. It'll also make for a tricky discussion if you design a news feed that runs against your interviewer's mental model of what it should look like. Design patterns are available for desktop, web and mobile user interfaces. Search Google for "web design patterns" or "mobile design patterns," and you'll find up-to-date resources on common design elements.

Practice Questions

1. Google shut down a location sharing service called Google Latitude on August 2013. How would you redesign and re-launch a location-sharing app?
2. Design a new iPad app for Google Spreadsheet.
3. How would you improve the LinkedIn mobile app?

Answers

Google shut down a location sharing service called Google Latitude on August 2013. How would you redesign and re-launch a location-sharing app?

CANDIDATE: Do you mind if I ask some clarifying questions?

INTERVIEWER: Sure.

CANDIDATE: My understanding is that Google Latitude allowed you to broadcast your location to your friends. And your friends could monitor your location, on a map, at all times.

INTERVIEWER: Yes, that's the basic gist.

CANDIDATE: Why did Google Latitude fail?

INTERVIEWER: Bad PR and poor adoption. The running joke was that the only people who liked the feature were jealous spouses and significant others. In other words, privacy was a big obstacle.

CANDIDATE: Why is Google interested in rebuilding the feature?

INTERVIEWER: There's a lot of potential with location sharing. From a user perspective, Google could improve its services if it knew where you were located. Google could provide relevant information, deals, and ads.

CANDIDATE: Okay, I have enough background information for now. Let me start by evaluating potential user personas. It sounds like monitoring is the key theme, so a few personas come to mind:

- Parents monitoring kids
- Pet owners monitoring pets
- Consumers monitoring packages
- Meeting participants monitoring arrival status of other attendees

INTERVIEWER: Can you elaborate more on each persona?

CANDIDATE: Sure, parents worry when they can't find their kids. If they knew where they were, they'd feel better. Pet owners have similar concerns.

Package delivery services offer tracking, but it's not in real-time or displayed on a map. If the consumer had a better sense of when a package would be delivered, they might be better prepared to be home when the delivery arrives.

Lastly, meeting participants would save time if they could monitor attendance. Many meetings are delayed because participants don't know the status of an important attendee. This same use case could also apply to restaurants, which need to make a decision whether to release a reservation to another waiting customer.

INTERVIEWER: Good. Of these use cases, which one are you most interested in?

CANDIDATE: I like the parent and pet owner use case. Both personas are constantly concerned about the safety of their kids and pets. This is a big problem, and they're willing to pay for a monitoring solution. I also like the restaurant use case because it could produce revenue. Anything that helps restaurants manage limited capacity is a win.

INTERVIEWER: Let's go with the parent use case. What would the solution look like?

CANDIDATE: I think the solution could be similar to Google Latitude. However, while many kids have smartphones, we can't assume that all kids have smartphones. Also, smartphones can easily be lost or left in backpacks.

I would design a watch that broadcasts a user's location and allows users to subscribe to their location feed. The location feed can be provided on a map, email or SMS. The kids wouldn't be able to turn off the broadcast.

INTERVIEWER: Doesn't this sound like Big Brother?

CANDIDATE: 24/7 monitoring does sound scary. But parents do 24/7 monitoring already, whether it's the incessant phone calls and texts to kids on where they are and what they're doing. And most parents do have authority. The kids might not like it, but some parents can get kids to do what they want.

Comments: The candidate did a great job of quickly scoping down to a relevant use case for this feature, which publishes a user's location to subscribers. He understood that the key value proposition (or as the candidate mentioned it, the theme) is monitoring. Once that was identified, he quickly narrowed it down to several personas that would find this monitoring value proposition useful.

Design a new iPad app for Google Spreadsheet.

CANDIDATE: Sure, I can design a new iPad app for Google Spreadsheet. Before I take a moment to brainstorm some ideas, can I ask a few clarifying questions?

INTERVIEWER: Sure.

CANDIDATE: What is the goal of creating this iPad app?

INTERVIEWER: What do you think might be our motivation to create one?

CANDIDATE: Well, the PC's share of total computing time is decreasing. More people are spending their time on mobile devices. Google would want to promote spreadsheet usage across those mobile devices. It would be a missed opportunity if Google allowed another competitor to become the leader in mobile spreadsheet applications.

INTERVIEWER: That's right. This is a defensive play.

CANDIDATE: Before I brainstorm ideas, do we have any constraints?

INTERVIEWER: We typically release new Google products on Android before iOS. However, in this case, we are short on Android developers, so we're going to do iOS first. And don't worry about time constraints. We'd rather get the product right than rush something to market.

CANDIDATE: Can I recruit Android developers to help?

INTERVIEWER: You can try, but let's just say that's a moot point for now.

CANDIDATE: I'm not familiar with the Google Spreadsheet customer base. Can you describe who they are, what they're trying to achieve, and what they would like to see in an iPad app?

INTERVIEWER: Why don't you tell me what you think it is?

CANDIDATE: I feel the Google Spreadsheet user likes Google Spreadsheet for a few reasons. First, all the documents are stored in the cloud, which means they can be revised on any machine without worrying about version control.

Second, it's very easy to collaborate. Multiple spreadsheet users can view and edit documents at the same time, meaning no more emailing attachments to each team member, asking them to make changes, and then compiling all the changes.

Lastly, it's free for anyone with a Google Account.

Google Spreadsheet doesn't have all the features of Microsoft Excel, so the spreadsheet is more likely to appeal to casual rather than expert users.

When it comes to casual users, many of them are spending more time with their mobile devices. They want to access their spreadsheets, which they can achieve through Google Drive or the browser. However, manipulating a spreadsheet is very cumbersome. Tapping cells to edit, typing formulas and selecting multiple cells—it's just not fun to do on a mobile device.

There might be some other use cases, such as the need for more powerful charting functionality and running sophisticated analyses like regression. But, it's not likely something our casual user base would care about. It also seems out of scope with the original question.

INTERVIEWER: You're correct. We want to build an iPad app that addresses the deficiencies of editing a spreadsheet in a mobile device. That's our top problem.

CANDIDATE: Okay, give me a moment to jot some ideas.

Candidate writes the following:

- *Voice input*
- *Gesture input*
- *Edit later on PC*

CANDIDATE: I have three suggestions to address the problem of editing a spreadsheet on a mobile device. The first idea is to have a voice input option that would allow the user to add the information or compute formulas by speaking.

The pros: voice input is fast and easy. The cons: voice recognition is not perfect and can be error-prone. It can also be embarrassing to use in a public place.

The second idea is gesture input. That is, create mobile device-friendly gestures to more easily manipulate a spreadsheet. For example, to add a column, the user can select the beginning and end of the column with his or her forefinger and thumb with a pinch motion. After the pinch motion, he or she can immediately draw a plus to indicate an addition operation, or draw an "X" to indicate a multiplication operation.

The advantage is that this uses multi-finger touchscreen technology for spreadsheet editing. The disadvantage is that the gestures are not intuitive or obvious. Significant training would have to occur, possibly burdening the user with sitting through a tutorial.

The third idea is to use an "edit later on PC" feature. On the mobile device, a user would be able to view spreadsheets and annotate changes to the spreadsheet. A simple one-click button sends a notification to the user the next time he or she is on the PC to make the changes.

The pros: changes are made in an environment where the user is comfortable and likely efficient. The cons: changes won't be made immediately. It adds an extra step to the process, leading to the likelihood that the user forgets or doesn't have time to make the changes the next time he or she uses a PC. This is my least favorite idea.

INTERVIEWER: Okay, I like those ideas. So which one do you think we should pursue first?

CANDIDATE: I would rule out the third idea, to begin with. It just doesn't sound effective and is not immediate.

I use Siri a lot, so voice input is intriguing. However, voice recognition might not be practical for manipulating a spreadsheet. Besides, I use Siri because I want to use my phone hands-free, like when I'm driving. I doubt anyone would or should edit a spreadsheet while driving a car.

That leaves us with a new gesture-based spreadsheet. I like that one. I think we can come up with some creative ways to build a spreadsheet that leverages the multi-gesture approach possible on touchscreen devices.

INTERVIEWER: Thanks for the recommendation.

Comments: The candidate covered all the salient points without making obvious that he is using a framework. It was an entertaining conversation as the candidate shared innovative and reasonable ideas.

How would you improve the LinkedIn mobile app?

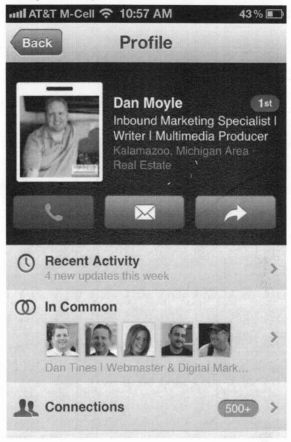

CANDIDATE: The LinkedIn mobile app has several features and pages. We don't have a lot of time, so let's pick a single page to focus on. Let's choose the user's profile page.

INTERVIEWER: Okay.

CANDIDATE: Let me review the page and see the key features: it's got the user photo, name, connection, title, geographic location and job industry. We have a few call-to-action buttons such as phone, email and share profile with others.

We can see the user's recent activity, connections we have in common and the user's connections.

For the redesign, my goal is to improve engagement on this page. Are there any other goals I should consider?

INTERVIEWER: No.

CANDIDATE: Putting myself into the mindset of a user, I like LinkedIn as a networking tool. It's an opportunity to find new business opportunities, either through new or existing connections.

Let's say Dan is someone I'm targeting for a business opportunity. When it comes to this particular opportunity, my biggest questions are:

- How can I get Dan to engage?
- What matters to Dan and why?

The second question is particularly important. If I know what is important to Dan, I can perhaps offer something of value. By showing value, Dan is more likely to reciprocate and participate in my business opportunity.

Give me a moment to collect my thoughts and see how I would redesign this page to capitalize on this insight.

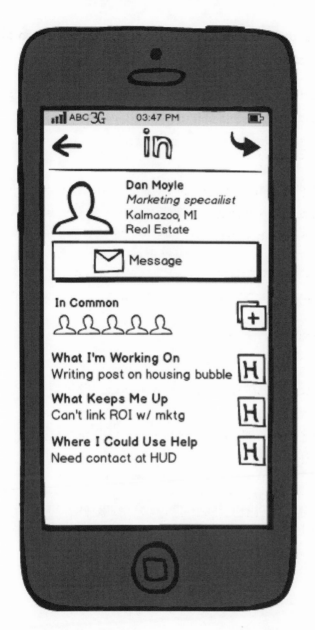

Okay, here's how I would re-design it. The top half is largely the same. I moved the share profile button to the upper right and removed the call button. The message button is significantly bigger, to emphasize the primary importance of this call-to-action.

The bottom half is completely redesigned. It shares three new information fields:

- **What I'm Working On**. It's a one-line field for the user to indicate their top deliverable for the day or week. In this case, we see that Dan is working on a blog post on the housing bubble.
- **What Keeps Me Up At Night**. This is another one-line field where the use can indicate their fears. In this case, Dan is concerned that he can't link his marketing efforts with the company's ROI goals. We can infer that this is about job security.
- **What I Could Use Help With**. This is the last one-line field where Dan can be specific on where he can use help. Sometimes people are unaware what help they need, so that's why the previous two fields are so critical.

What I love about this solution is that it greatly increases the opportunities for business development. What I don't like about this solution is that it requires the user to be proactive about updating their status messages. We won't get 100 percent compliance.

Comments: Candidate does a good job using the primary persona and thinking through what is an inhibitor for more business development opportunities on LinkedIn. This idea is deceptively powerful; it's almost like Twitter's introduction of a 140-character message within LinkedIn.

Chapter 5 Designing a Consumer Product

Apply the same CIRCLES Method™ when asked to design a consumer product.

Tip: Don't Blindly Follow Frameworks

Whether it's the CIRCLES Method™ or a different design framework, don't blindly follow it. It'll sound scripted. Not too long ago, a product management candidate started the design interview with, "First, I want to understand the product. Second, I want to talk about potential customers. Third, I want talk about their needs. Fourth, I will prioritize their needs. Fifth, I will brainstorm solutions. Sixth, I will evaluate tradeoffs. Seventh, I will make my recommendation."

Interviewers will react to candidates that sound robotic. Some will label the person as over prepared. Others, like me, would fear that the candidate is inexperienced. Inexperienced candidates lack confidence. They are more likely to strictly follow a prescribed framework.

Contrast the previous response with the following: "I'm not too familiar with the product. Can you tell me more about it? That's fascinating. I can see why they would find feature X valuable. However, it doesn't quite sound like the product meets their needs. Do you mind if I explore that in more detail?"

This sounds like a conversation I could have with a co-worker. The candidate also seems polished and confident. The interview is about establishing credibility and likability. Interviewers don't like robots. They like candidates that have personality and are similar to the interviewer.

One last thing, the interviewer is looking for problem solvers who can think critically. Frameworks are meant to be a memory aid. Adapt to your specific interview question.

Interviewers can tell when you used a hammer when a scalpel would have sufficed. Use and trust your own judgment and you'll be amazed how natural your responses will be. You'll also have more fun when you're not straining to parrot a technique you learned from a book.

Practice Question

1. Re-design a garage door opener.

Answer

Re-design a garage door opener.

CANDIDATE: Is this for residential or commercial?

INTERVIEWER: Residential.

CANDIDATE: And what's the goal of the re-design? Increase market share? Increase revenue?

INTERVIEWER: Your boss is the owner of a garage door company. Garage doors haven't really evolved much over the last few decades. He feels a redesign of the garage door opener could lead to differentiation and more market share for the company.

CANDIDATE: I'll start by exploring the user problems. When I think about the problems, a few come to mind:

1. The garage door opens slowly. Maybe it doesn't take this long, but it feels like it takes 10-15 seconds to open or close.
2. Sometimes, I'm not sure if the garage door closed. When I'm away from home, there's that nagging feeling that it might still be open.

3. Lastly, the garage door opener is an extra device. I feel like I should be able to open and close the garage door with the device I do carry with myself all the time, my smartphone.

I'd like to brainstorm a couple of solutions.

The first idea addresses use case number 3. That is, open your garage door using your smartphone. The garage door could be connected to a wireless network, and a smartphone app could automatically open and close the garage door. The benefit is that the user no longer needs an extra electronic device to open the garage door. The downside is that this wouldn't serve those that don't have smartphones. Good news is that American smartphone penetration is nearly 60 percent and growing. Another downside is smartphone connectivity might not be reliable. The local wireless network and cellular data introduces additional points of failure.

The second idea addresses use case number 2. Provide an SMS, email or in-app confirmation on whether the garage door closed. The app could also monitor the state of the garage door and provide alerts when the garage door is open. This will be especially valuable, especially during times when the garage door should be closed, such as during the working day. There are no true cons to this idea; it's better than constant worrying or waiting 10-15 seconds for the garage door to close before leaving the house.

The third idea addresses use case number 1. We could include a timer function where the garage door would automatically open at preset times and days. While this alleviates the "waiting for 10-15 seconds" problem, this could be an issue, especially when it opens on days when it doesn't need to be open. Or it automatically closes when a child is underneath. It seems better to simply have the garage door open and close on demand.

INTERVIEWER: Okay, so what would you recommend?

CANDIDATE: I would recommend doing ideas number 1 and 2.

Comments: The candidate does a good job of clarifying the objective and the situation. The use cases are detailed. The candidate offers three solid feature suggestions.

Chapter 6 Designing a Service or Other Product

Apply the same CIRCLES Method™ when asked to design service or other products.

Tip: Ask the Five Whys to Understand Unarticulated Problems

As part of understanding customer needs, you may have to delve into a customer's workflow with their existing solutions. To find areas of improvement, you'll have to understand obstacles they are facing and gaps that existing solutions have left open.

Here's an easy way to determine gaps: ask the "Five Whys." This is a technique popularized by the carmaker Toyota. It involves iterative inquiry to identify a problem's root cause. In this case, we'll use it diagnose problems with processes, proposed innovations and existing customer solutions.

Five Whys Example

Question	Answer and the corresponding issue
Why does the production line close down every third Sunday?	We have to clean the equipment.
Why do we have to clean the equipment?	Dirt and dust will damage critical parts, leading to more downtime if it must be replaced.
Why does cleaning take all day?	We have to disassemble the machine part by part and then clean all the internal parts.
Why can't we reduce the cleaning time?	We could if we simply put an inexpensive aluminum foil on the parts that get dirty often.
Why haven't covered the easily dirty parts with aluminum foil?	We can't get the procurement department to approve the purchase.

Practice Questions

1. Assume you are the new product manager in our Amazon Prime business and are in charge of feature development. What data would you look at to develop new features? What new features would they be?
2. The billboard industry is under monetized. How can Google create a new product or offering to address this?

Answers

Assume you are the new product manager in our Amazon Prime business and are in charge of feature development. What data would you look at to develop new features? What new features would they be?

CANDIDATE: Before we jump into the question, do you mind if I clarify my understanding of Amazon Prime, especially the service and the benefits to both the customer and to Amazon's overall business.

INTERVIEWER: Sure.

CANDIDATE: I understand that Amazon Prime is a membership club. Amazon Prime members get free two-day shipping for every order they place. They can also stream movies & TV shows for free and borrow books from the Kindle library.

Correct me if I'm wrong, I believe the biggest benefit for Prime members is shipping. Normally, free super saver shipping takes five to eight days to arrive. Two day shipping is a big improvement. By making it available to all orders, Amazon Prime's two-day shipping benefit likely reduces indecision around whether to upgrade from Free Super Saver to a one-time shipping upgrade.

I've heard Amazon Prime helps the business because:

- Customers order more frequently.
- Customers spend more.
- Customers buy products that they wouldn't otherwise buy at Amazon.
- It leverages Amazon's competitive advantage, an ultra-fast fulfillment process.
- Customers have high satisfaction.
- It steals wallet share from competitors.

Okay, so back to the question. If I were to develop new features, I'd start with our business goal. What are we trying to achieve? Our goal can include any of the aforementioned metrics:

- Increase sales per Prime customer
- Increase in the number of Prime customers
- Increase Prime customer satisfaction

Let's say the goal is to increase the number of new Prime customers. I've heard that Amazon has approximately 30 million customers, with anywhere from 5 to 30 percent opted into the Prime program.

We would need to investigate why regular Amazon customers won't try Amazon Prime. It could be for several reasons:

- They aren't aware of it.
- They aren't interested or don't see the value in it.
- They are interested but not willing to make the effort.
- They tried it, but aren't compelled to pay for it.

Based on your knowledge, what's the primary reason why customers don't try Amazon Prime?

INTERVIEWER: 65 percent of Amazon customers are aware of Amazon Prime, but only half of that group has paid for it. The reason they haven't paid: they didn't find the value proposition compelling.

CANDIDATE: Thanks for the insight. Unless you disagree, let's assume that marketing is not the reason why there's not enough interest. Putting that out of scope allows us to focus on our discussion on developing new product and program features.

INTERVIEWER: Okay.

CANDIDATE: When it comes to developing new features, I'd like to see data on customer's top pain points with his or her Amazon shopping experience. Then we'll construct new Prime features to address the top pain point. Off the top of my head, I feel these are the top Amazon customer pain points:

- Can't find the product I need
- Not a bargain
- Not timely
- Too much of a hassle to buy online

Okay, I'll go ahead with that "can't find the product I need" use case. Give me a moment to brainstorm some ideas.

Candidate takes 60 seconds to brainstorm

CANDIDATE: I have a few features in mind to solve that problem:

- Personal shopper
- Free return shipping
- Product perks club

Personal shopper gives each Prime member customized help when shopping for products. They provide customized gift ideas, research products and help navigate Amazon's seemingly endless database.

Customer satisfaction and purchases are likely to go up — existing Prime members. The downside is that this concierge would be costly.

Free return shipping gives an assurance that if they buy the wrong product they can easily return it later, without incurring additional shipping costs. This may lead to new Prime customers, but it also increases costs for not only new Prime customers but also old Prime customers.

Product perks club is a special club where customers are invited to sample or test products and write reviews. This introduces the Prime member to new products and makes them feel special. The cost may be partially subsidized by manufacturers, who may want to get their products in front of Amazon customers.

Of all the feature ideas presented, I feel that product perks club has the best benefits and also has minimal cost. Customers and advertisers will like it. The costs could be manageable, especially if subsidized by advertisers.

However, the feature that could have the most impact is the free return shipping. The inability to return is what I feel is a big barrier to driving more purchases from brick-and-mortar to online. Free return shipping could lead to a significant group of new Amazon Prime customers.

Comments: The candidate gives a good response that indicates a solid understanding of the product, why adoption is low and what suggestions would improve adoption. However, the candidate doesn't explicitly cite the metrics he would look at. He suggests some features, which don't appear to be too creative. For instance, one of the ideas, Products Perks Club, sounds a little too similar to

, which makes new and pre-release products
reviewers. The reviewers get to keep those
ving them.

stry is under monetized. How
a new product or offering to
address this?

CANDIDATE: Okay, you want me to design a new product that will change the billboard industry. Analyzing why the billboard industry is under monetized is out of scope, correct?

INTERVIEWER: You got it.

Candidate writes on the whiteboard

Customer problems

- *Ads are irrelevant*
- *Ads are static*
- *Ads have poor recall*

CANDIDATE: Okay, I always start with the user. In this case, it's the commuter who sees the billboards. There are a couple of challenges:

1. First, not all billboards are relevant. When I drive up and down the 101, there are many billboards focused on technology enterprises. These billboards aren't relevant to all commuters.
2. Second, billboards don't change. There's a missed opportunity to add more information on a billboard, especially if a user is stuck in traffic and has time to read more.
3. Third, it's hard to remember the contents of a billboard. If I want to research or follow-up on the advertised company, it's tough. The web address, phone number, even the name —

these are things I'd like to remember, but can't because I'm focused on driving.

INTERVIEWER: How would you solve these problems?

CANDIDATE: Give me a moment to brainstorm.

30 second pause

CANDIDATE: Let's start with the second use case. We can upgrade the billboards to rotate through different ads. There are electronic billboards today, but I've found the ad rotation is typically limited. Google can expand the ad rotation by:

- **Bring new advertisers**. Introduce its advertisers to billboard advertising, a new platform for many.
- **Introduce new ad formats and layouts**, including multiple ads on a single billboard.
- **Offer a real-time ad auction system**. I presume that billboard ads are sold on a monthly basis, which limits ad competition and variety. By allowing advertisers to compete for ad space in real-time, it would increase the ads available for rotation.
- **Offer targeting opportunities**

INTERVIEWER: What kind of targeting opportunities would you offer?

CANDIDATE: Obvious targeting options include location, time of day and day of week. Target could get more advanced. We could target based on weather or traffic patterns. Just imagine an ad that's relevant: "Stay in this traffic and get back home by 8 p.m. Get a $10 day pass at 24 Hour Fitness, work out, let the traffic die down and you'll get home by 8:30 p.m."

INTERVIEWER: How would the real-time ad auction work?

CANDIDATE: This would be similar to how Google AdWords and online ad exchanges work. Give advertisers the opportunity to bid on every single impression available in Google's inventory. By making bidding real-time, it allows advertisers pay more for targeted impressions that count and less for impressions that don't.

INTERVIEWER: Okay, how about the other two use cases?

CANDIDATE: For the first use case, advertising relevancy, the aforementioned targeting options will make more advertising more relevant. But I feel Google can take it one step further.

For example, Google has developed a core competence around computer vision through Google's driverless cars. It's not a stretch for Google to adapt computer vision to recognize cars on the road. For instance, it can detect a Black Lexus SUV or recognize letters on a license plate.

Based on that data, Google can show an ad appropriate to that driver or cluster of drivers. For example, a group of commuters who drive luxury cars are more likely to respond to an ad about an exotic Mediterranean vacation.

INTERVIEWER: Unique idea, but wouldn't that be controversial?

CANDIDATE: You mean target ads based on a license plate number?

INTERVIEWER: Yes.

CANDIDATE: I agree that there are privacy implications and that's something that would have to be researched. We would have to develop well thought out talking points before the feature goes to market.

INTEVIEWER: Okay, how about the third use case?

CANDIDATE: We could create a billboard search engine to help commuters recall billboards. Users can enter a company name and location. Or we could make it more advanced. Perhaps users can browse through a shortlist of billboard ads based on the user's recent travels, garnered from smartphone GPS chip data. Or perhaps we can offer a voice-recognition feature on smartphones to bookmark billboards during a drive.

These recall solutions aren't perfect, but they're better than other ideas I've considered which include asking the user to take a picture of the billboard as well as memorize a website or offer code. Those ideas are either too difficult or distracting for the user who is driving.

Comments: Our candidate offers an excellent response. He starts by recounting user challenges in detail. He thinks big by offering ideas like targeted advertising based on car make and model as well as license plate. It has the makings of a big idea: unique, memorable, seemingly farfetched, but upon further explanation seems plausible. Overall, his response is very creative and thoughtful.

Chapter 7 Getting Technical

Nothing gets the product manager's heart pumping than the technical interview. A technical interview is asked to explain a technical concept, propose a technical algorithm, solve a programming interview question or describe technical implementation of a product.

Not all companies have a technical portion to their interview. Ask the recruiter, hiring manager or friends at a particular company on whether you should prepare for a technical interview. For example, expect a technical interview if you reach an on-site interview at Google.

Why does Google care whether or not their PMs are technically proficient? Google PMs are expected to lead engineers. A technically-fluent product manager will garner respect from engineers.

How to Approach a Technical Interview Question

When tackling a technical interview question, there are a couple steps to keep in mind:

1. **Understand what is being asked**. If necessary, ask to clarify the goal and the problem statement.
2. **Work through the simple base case**. The solution and the accompanying clarifying questions will be more apparent as you work through it.
3. **Talk aloud**. It'll help the interviewer understand where you're headed. The interviewer may even intervene and provide helpful guidance.
4. **Write the technical solution, if necessary**. For most organizations, they don't expect the syntax to be perfect; pseudo code is fine.

5. **Review the code**. Evaluate the strengths and weaknesses. Revise as necessary. Few can write code without bugs in the first pass.

We've shared some simple technical questions here. However, I also recommend reviewing core computer science concepts, such as sorting algorithms, trees and hash tables. Then practice the same coding questions companies would ask entry-level software engineers. Companies like Google understand that you may be rusty, but they do want you to attempt the technical interview question.

Practice Questions

1. Brainstorm as many algorithms as possible for recommending Twitter followers.
2. Explain recursion.
3. Explain object-oriented programming to your grandmother.
4. How would you reduce Gmail's storage size?
5. How would you design a blogging application?
6. You're part of the Google Search web spam team. How would you detect duplicate websites?
7. Write an algorithm that detects meeting conflicts.
8. Design an elevator control system.
9. There's a server bottleneck. How would you solve it?

Answers

Brainstorm as many algorithms as possible for recommending Twitter followers.

CANDIDATE: Okay, give me one moment to think about this.

Candidate jots down the following:

- *Actions: view or follow*
- *View relationships: stalker or mutual acquaintances*
- *Follow states: following, being followed or mutual following*

CANDIDATE: When I mull this problem, I think of behaviors, relationships and states.

For behavior, I think about whether a Twitter user views another's profile or if a Twitter user follows another.

I will consider two view-based relationships. If a user views the other, but the other user does not view back despite a suggestion, we'll call that a stalker relationship. However, if both individuals view one another when suggested, it's likely they know each other. We'll call that an acquaintance relationship.

Lastly, for the following states, there are three scenarios I see. First, the viewer follows the one being viewed, but not the other way around. Second, the viewed follows the viewer, but not the other way around. Third, both follow the other.

To summarize, on Twitter, there are two view relationships:

- Stalker: A views B. B does not view A.
- Acquaintances: A views B. B views A.

Here's a visual representation of these relationships:

	A views B	A does not view B
B views A	Acquaintances	Stalker
B does not view A	Stalker	No relation

We can improve the algorithm to suggest a third user C – to either user A or B – depending on A and B's relationship to C and each other.

The table below visually represents the permutations:

	A following C	A followed by C	A acquaintance of C
B followed by C	A > C > B	A < C > B	A <> C > B
B following C	A > C < B	A < C < B	A <> C < B
B acquaintance of C	A > C <> B	A < C <> B	A <> C <> B

INTERVIEWIER: Okay, you've indicated 11 different algorithm options. Which one would you choose?

CANDIDATE: Well, I would implement all the algorithms, run A/B tests, and see which one has the best suggestion-to-follow ratio. But I believe you're asking me to prioritize which one I would like to try first.

The one I like best is A <> C <> B. That is, if A is an acquaintance with C and B is an acquaintance with C, then it's very likely that A and B are likely to be acquaintances too. It's a phenomena modeled on real life. That is, assuming C knows A and B well, at some point C would introduce A and B to each other.

INTERVIEWER: Thanks for the recommendation.

Comments: Candidate was organized and exhaustive in evaluating attributes and states for a recommendation engine. The A/B test suggestion shows that he's also objective, unbiased and willing to experiment.

Explain recursion.

CANDIDATE: Outside of work, I've been teaching computer programming to eighth-grade kids in East Palo Alto. Two weeks ago, I taught them a new programming concept called recursion. I introduced it with Wikipedia's definition:

Recursion is a method where the solution to a problem depends on solutions to smaller instances of the same problem.

As you can imagine, their eyes glazed over. I could explain by writing some code below, but I don't think it would have helped.

Candidate writes the following on the whiteboard.

```
unsigned int factorial(unsigned int n) {

  if (n == 0) {

    return 1;

  } else {

    return n * factorial(n - 1);

  }

}
```

Then, I remembered an answer I read on Quora. It used a movie theater analogy to explain recursion.

Inspired by that example, I told the students,

"Let's say you're in a movie theater where the rows are not numbered. Someone asks you which row you're in. You don't want to count, so you ask the person in front of you. He doesn't want to count either, so they ask the person in front of them.

This continues all the way to the person in the front row. That person doesn't see anyone in front of them, so they tell the person behind them that he's in the 1st row. The guy in the 2nd row adds 1 to his response and tells the person behind him that he's in the 3rd row.

This continues all the way back to the person who originally asked the question."

The example worked. The students understood the concept by affirming that the question "What row am I?" can be rephrased (recursively) as "How many people are in front of me + 1?" with a base case of zero. Some students even recognized that requests could be pushed on and off the stack. Most importantly, I was proud that the youngsters grasped a concept that many college students struggle with.

Comments: Example is a tough concept. Response shows three alternatively ways to answering. The candidate clearly demonstrates that his way was better.

Explain object-oriented programming to your grandmother.

CANDIDATE: I'll start by answering what is object-oriented programming (OOP).

OOP organizes computer code into objects. This is different from conventional programming, where programs are just a sequence of tasks. The main idea is objects vs. tasks.

I'll give an example. Let's say we're programming a racing video game. There are several different cars in the game.

We can program an object called a "car." The car object has a state and operations:

The car's state can include current speed, brake on and off, and steering direction.

The car's operations can include accelerate, brake, and steer.

Let's say the first car in the game is a Toyota. Now, if we want a BMW, we don't need to create a brand new car from scratch. We can just derive the new BMW based on the basic car object, because the BMW, like all car objects can do three things: accelerate, brake and steer. And the BMW car can add its own special properties such as a windshield wiper that automatically adjusts its speed based on how heavy the rain is.

Why do we need OOP? There are a couple reasons why we do this. First, it saves time. If we already have a car object, we don't need to program identical functionality multiple times. Second, the object metaphor is easy to understand. It's easy to communicate to others the idea of creating objects and that the object is capable of doing actions that another object might not. Lastly, this programming convention keeps it organized. For example, a Ford Mustang convertible should rightly have the ability to remove the vinyl top, while the Toyota Prius should not. By limiting the vinyl top removal action to the Ford Mustang convertible object, we limit unintended actions by the Toyota Prius.

Comments: The reason the interviewer is asking this question because they want to test your understanding of technical concepts. She also wants you to prove your ability to communicate difficult concepts to different audiences. The candidate's response is factually correct while tastefully leaving out advanced and potentially confusing details, such as encapsulation and polymorphism. It uses sufficient detail to explain the central idea around OOP, inheritance. It addresses the listener's main objection to OOP using overriding.

How would you reduce Gmail's storage size?

CANDIDATE: Give me a moment to brainstorm some ideas.

Candidate writes the following in his notes:

- *Compression*
- *Deletion*
- *Client-side storage*

- *Off-site storage*

	Description	Pros	Cons	Mitigation
Compression strategy 1	Apply a compression algorithm	More space	Slower access; likely doing this already	Selectively choose messages
Compression strategy 2	Concatenate files then compress	More space	Slower access	Selectively choose messages
Deletion	(Self-explanatory)	More space	Can't auto delete messages, goes against Gmail marketing	Quotas, overage charge, auto-delete after X days
Single item storage	Keep single copy of email, images, and attachments that is included in multiple emails	More space	N/A	
Client-side storage	Store some emails on client machine	More space	Can't access all messages everywhere	Selectively choose messages
Off-site storage	Store some emails on off-site storage	Lower cost	Slower access times	Selectively choose messages

CANDIDATE: I've thought of at least 4 different ways Gmail can save storage space.

Candidate walks to the whiteboard.

CANDIDATE: Let me describe each one, and I'll talk about the pros and cons for each.

Candidate then describes the table above, in detail.

Comments: To answer the question well, use the design framework, but skip the customer problem, personas, and prioritization. Skip directly to brainstorming solutions. The interviewer is looking for you to generate many solutions. She is also looking for rigor in your pro/con analysis. The interviewer is also evaluating the candidate's technical understanding. Don't forget to ask clarifying questions in the beginning.

How would you design a blogging application?

CANDIDATE: Are you asking me to develop a blogging application for the web, desktop or mobile application?

INTERVIEWER: Website.

CANDIDATE: And are you looking for the UI or something else?

INTERVIEWER: I want you to specify the data model and key functions. Then I want you to walk my through how those functions get called.

CANDIDATE: I'd start by creating the data model. There are a couple of things we would need to store:

Blog post data model

- Blog post number
- Title
- Body content
- Entry date

Comments data model

- Comment number
- Comment name
- Comment author's email

- Body content
- Entry date

Then, I'd create a few functions:

- GetAllPosts()
- GetSinglePost()
  - o GetComments()
- AddNewEntry()
- ShowSinglePost()
  - o AddComment()
- ShowAllPosts()

I'll walk you through how all this comes together.

- The user visits the blog home page. This calls GetAllPosts(), which gets the last 10 blog posts in reverse chronological order.
- Once the data is retrieved, ShowAllPosts() puts the information in the appropriate view, which includes the HTML rendered in the user's brow.
- A user can click to see a specific blog post. This calls GetSinglePost() and a subroutine, GetComments() which retrieves that specific blog post and comments from the database.
- Once the data is retrieved, ShowSinglePost() puts the information in the appropriate view.
- If the user decides to add a comment, it calls AddComment(), which saves the author's comment to the database, after appropriate authentication.

Comments: This is not a particularly difficult question. It does test the candidate's comfort level discussing technical details. The

candidate does a solid job specifying the basic data model, core functions and a walkthrough of user input interacts with each part of the program.

You're part of the Google Search web spam team. How would you detect duplicate websites?

INTERVIEWER: People are copying content across websites. Develop an algorithm to determine which one is the original and which one is the copied one.

CANDIDATE: Give me a moment to brainstorm some solutions.

Here are the solutions that come to mind:

- Apply a hash function (#) to the content; subsequent pages with similar content are duplicates.
- Content with the most hashes of inbound links is the original.
- Embed a unique ID to a page. Ensuing pages without a unique ID, but with the same content, are duplicates.
- Compare timestamps for similar webpages; assume earlier one is the original one.
- Factor domain reputation. Domains that are known to copy original content are penalized.

Here are the pros and cons of each solution:

Solution	Risks
Apply a hash function; subsequent ones are duplicates.	Google may incorrectly process the copied page before the original page.
Content with the most number of inbound links is the original.	Bad actors can setup a content farm, inflate the number of links and game the system.
Embed a unique ID to a page.	This would require additional work for webmasters. Also, there may not be 100 percent compliance.

Compare timestamps for webpages; assume the page with the earlier time stamp is the newer one.	Webmasters can fake early timestamps.
Domain reputation	Penalizing domains with a history of copying original content could require manual intervention, which is slow and costly.

Given the pros and cons, I recommend that we apply the following solutions: do hash function, unique ID, and domain reputation.

Comments: The candidate generates a large number of potential solutions. The pro and con analysis is thoughtful. He concludes with a set of recommendations.

Write an algorithm that detects meeting conflicts.

CANDIDATE: Let me work through a simple example and then I'll write the code to address any case.

Let's say the first meeting starts at 9 a.m. and ends at 11 a.m. The shorthand would be:

- S1 (start of first meeting): 9 a.m.
- E1 (end of first meeting): 11 a.m.

There's a conflict if the 2nd meeting starts before 11 a.m. or ends after 9 a.m. Representing this in shorthand:

- S2 < E1
- E2 > S1

To help visualize this:

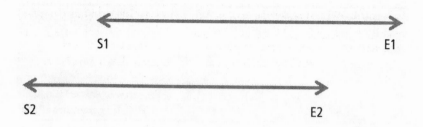

S1   E1

S2   E2

We can represent the (S2 < E1 or E2 > S1) logic in our code below.

```
bool IsConflict(Datetime s1, Datetime e1, Datetime s2, Datetime e2) {

    return (s1 < e2) || (e1 > s2);

}
```

Comments: This is an easy algorithm question that can inspire fear into a product management candidate. As long as the candidate can calm their nerves and take a moment to understand the situation, the candidate will realize that a single one-line logic statement provides the answer.

Design an elevator control system.

INTERVIEWER: I'd like you to design a control algorithm for an elevator system.

CANDIDATE: Do you mean an algorithm for how to respond to incoming passenger requests and the corresponding elevator actions?

INTERVIEWER: Yes, that's correct.

CANDIDATE: Sure, give me a moment to brainstorm.

Candidate pauses for 60 seconds

Approach	Description	Analysis

First come first served (FCFS)	Process passengers as they arrive	Minimize latency with little regard to throughput
Shortest seek time first (SSTF)	Process passengers from the floor that is closest	Elevator moving time is minimized. Will have better throughput than FCFS, but request may be delayed if many closely related passengers arrive after it
SCAN	Visit top floor before changing direction and sweeping back to first floor	Movement time is minimized and fairer than SSTF
Circular SCAN (C-SCAN)	Visit top floor, don't pick up any passengers on the way back to the 1st floor, and start picking up passengers again	Fairer performance than SCAN because middle floors don't get serviced twice as often
LOOK	Similar to SCAN, elevator makes use of information about locations requested. For example, as elevator moves to the top floor, the elevator will reverse if there are no waiting requests for locations beyond the current floor.	Movement time is minimized
C-LOOK	Similar to LOOK and C-SCAN	Movement time is minimized with benefit of C-SCAN

CANDIDATE: Here are some algorithms I brainstormed. I'll explain algorithm and then discuss the pros and cons of each.

Candidate walks the interviewer through the table above

Comments: Candidate appropriately clarifies the question and then brainstorms a comprehensive list. Well done.

There's a server bottleneck. How would you solve it?

INTERVIEWER: If you had a server (like SharePoint) in the US that stored your client's insurance information and your colleagues wanted to access and update these docs but have been complaining about the long wait times and network disconnections, how would you approach this?

CANDIDATE: I haven't analyzed server bottlenecks since college. Do you mind if I ask a few clarifying questions?

INTERVIEWER: Okay.

CANDIDATE: When it comes to slow response times for a SharePoint site, I can think of several causes: network, server, storage, database, application latency.

Network latency can be caused by slow or overloaded network connections at the data center or the end user's location. A slow Internet backbone can also be the cause of network latency.

Server latency is caused by slow processors and inefficient server hardware architectures.

Storage latency is due to slow performing storage devices. Solid state drives and in-memory solutions offer higher performance.

Database (DB) latency occurs when the application makes frequent database trips. DB latency can be especially challenging when it's being used to store binary data when DBs are meant to store relational data.

Applications are inefficiently slow if they use suboptimal data structures and poor algorithms. Applications can also be unnecessarily slow, if they run on operating systems that aren't optimized for the latest hardware. Lastly SharePoint applications can be slow if there are deadlock scenarios.

INTERVIEWER: Thanks for your preliminary diagnosis. Let's continue the hypothetical situation. Let's say the IT team has ruled out network, server, storage, and application latency. They've isolated it to database latency. What next?

CANDIDATE: One of the options to solving the database latency is to use a different backend for SharePoint. Many companies are now using NoSQL solutions such as MongoDB to store non-relational data. Unfortunately, the last time I checked, SharePoint does not support NoSQL, even Windows Azure Tables, Microsoft's version of NoSQL.

Another solution is to migrate SharePoint binary data into documents that are stored on a file system or SAN/NAS storage. This minimizes DB trips and DB latency.

The last suggestion I have is to utilize an in-memory distributed cache. This would alleviate database traffic with a cache system that's optimized for read operations.

Comments: Candidate offers a comprehensive answer that indicates familiarity with server issues. One suggestion for improvement: make it sound less formal and a little more casual.

Chapter 8 Getting Analytical: Estimation

Estimation questions have been incorrectly labeled as brainteasers, primarily because some estimation questions seem too corny to be taken seriously. Here are some classic favorites:

- How many golf balls can fit a school bus?
- How much does a 747 weigh?

Look past the wacky packaging; estimation questions have real world practicality. Product managers make decisions all the time: whether to respond to a customer complaint on feature A vs. B or how many servers to order for a new service. It's a judgment call and that judgment is based on the product manager's estimate of a metric.

Interviewers also use estimation questions to evaluate your listening and problem solving skills. They're seeing whether or not you can identify critical assumptions and your judgment in choosing assumptions. It wouldn't make sense if I claimed that a 747 weighs 1,000 pounds, would it?

There are two ways to answer estimation questions: top down and bottoms up.

Top Down Estimation Method

The top down approach starts with the whole and working its way down to the parts. For instance, to estimate sales of an Xbox console, a top down approach would start from the total available market — that is, anyone who can afford an Xbox. In this case, a candidate might start with the U.S. population, a little over 315 million, then hone in on the target market, which is a subset of the available market.

Bottom Up Estimation Method

The bottom up approach hinges on observations. That is, collect a single data point and then assume that what's true for a single data point can be assumed for the data point in question. For instance, if we are trying to estimate iPhone sales in the United States, we might start by visiting a single Apple store in New York City. With a clipboard in hand, we might ask outgoing customers whether they bought an iPhone. After an hour's worth of data, we can make inferences on how many iPhones are sold in the store in a given day, month or year. And from there, we can infer sales across all Apples stores in the United States.

Practice Questions

1. Estimate McDonald's revenue.
2. How many queries per second does Gmail get?
3. How many iPhones are sold in the US each year?
4. Estimate how much it costs to run Flickr for a 20 GB user.
5. How many elevators do you need for a 50-story building?

Answers

Estimate McDonald's revenue.

CANDIDATE: For this question, are you expecting an actual number or did you want me to just talk through how I'd find this number in real life?

INTERVIEWER: I don't question your ability to find the number in McDonald's SEC filings. Instead, I want you to provide a back-of-the-envelope estimate.

CANDIDATE: And to clarify, are you looking for McDonald's annual U.S. revenue?

INTERVIEWER: Annual revenue yes. But I want the international revenue number.

CANDIDATE: Okay, here's how I'll approach the question. I'll do a bottom-up approach. I'll first estimate the revenue of a single McDonald's store here in the U.S., and then I'll multiply that number by the number of U.S. stores. Finally, I'll extrapolate the U.S. revenue number to an international number.

Okay, go for it.

CANDIDATE: When I think about a single McDonald's, I believe most McDonalds' are open 24 hours or at least from 7 a.m., to 11 p.m.

I believe that McDonald's busy hours are 8 a.m., to 8 p.m. every day. During these peak times, there are 50 to 80 groups of customers per hour. If we take the midpoint of the range, we get 65 groups. A group of customers could be a single person or even a family of four. Let's say on average its two people. 65 times 2 equal 130 customers per hour.

Kids usually order happy meals, which retail for $5. Adults usually get a combo, which retails for $8. Let's say the average revenue per customer is $7. $7 average revenue times 130 is $910 per hour.

The busy period is about 12 hours in length. Multiple 12 times $910 per hour. We get $10,920 during peak hours. Let's say that a typical McDonald's store makes 15 percent of its revenue out of peak hours. Thus, during the whole day a typical McDonald's makes $12,847.

Extrapolate that over the course of a year and a single McDonald's makes $4.7 million.

Now to estimate McDonald's U.S. revenue, we need to factor in the number of stores. I live in Seattle, and there are probably 10

McDonald's. Seattle is one of the bigger cities in the US. I'd estimate the typical US city only has 3 McDonalds.

As for the number of cities in the United States, there are 50 states. Each state must have at least 100 cities. So that's 5,000 cities. 5,000 cities multiplied by 3 McDonalds' per city; that gives us 15,000 McDonalds.

Multiple 15,000 by annual revenue of $4.7 million, and we get $70.5B per year.

For many companies, like Google, U.S. revenue is approximately half the total revenue. If we use similar assumptions, the worldwide McDonald's revenue is $141B.

INTERVIEWER: In 2008, the average McDonald's store makes about $3 million per year. Why do you think your estimate is off?

CANDIDATE: I likely overestimated the number of customers per hour. In retrospect, McDonald's is really busiest around lunchtime. I probably should have shaved off twenty to thirty percent the number of customers going into a McDonald's.

Comments: Candidate did a good job with a bottom up approach for the revenue estimate. The candidate asked the right clarifying questions, gave a brief overview of approach, multiplied numbers in a way that was easy to follow and gave a reasonable estimate.

How many queries per second does Gmail get?

CANDIDATE: Do I get any additional background information?

INTERVIEWER: Nope, that's it. I'm waiting for your number.

CANDIDATE: Okay, I'm going to define a query as a Gmail operation. It could be a read, write or search operation.

First, I'm going to estimate the number of Gmail users. Then, I'll estimate how often they use the service and how many operations they perform.

INTERVIEWER: Go on.

CANDIDATE: Starting from the top and working our way down: there are approx. 7 billion people in the world. Internet usage in developed countries is likely to be in the 70 to 80 percent range. However, it's much lower for developing countries. So I'll assume that 40 percent of 7 billion people, or 2.8 billion people use the Internet.

The next number I need is the percentage of people that use Gmail as their primary account. When I think about my friends, I'd say about 70 percent use Gmail as their primary account. I know several that use other services. Given that my friends are more tech-savvy and American-centric than others, let's say worldwide only 20 percent use Gmail as their primary account. That gives us 560 million Gmail primary users.

I log into my Gmail account multiple times a day, but let's say the average Gmail user logs into their account about 4 times a week. Each time they login, let's say they read on average eight emails, compose two emails and search for one email. Thus, the number of queries is:

(4 Gmail logins per week) x ([8 read email operations per login] + [2 compose email operations per login] + [1 search email operation]) = 44 Gmail queries per week per user

CANDIDATE: Finally, to get number of Gmail queries per second, we do the following math:

(560 million Gmail users) * (44 Gmail operations per week per user) * (1 week per 604,800 seconds) = 40.7k queries per second

CANDIDATE: There are approximately 41k Gmail queries per second.

Comments: Candidate does well, especially since the interviewer hasn't been too helpful. Methodology is reasonable, and the calculations are easy to follow.

How many iPhones are sold in the US each year?

CANDIDATE: For this question, I'd like to start with stating assumptions and then doing my top down calculations.

Starting with the assumptions:

- There are approximately 315 million people in the United States.
- 90 percent of people have a cell phone.
- Cell phone users are locked into contracts. That is, they cannot get a new phone unless they pay a penalty to break a contract. The contract is normally two years, so cell phones get replaced once every two years.
- Each person buys on average 1 cell phone.
- Smartphones are about 60 percent of new cell phone sales.
- The iPhone has 40 percent market share of the smartphone market.

Going into the calculations:

The number of people looking to buy a new phone each year is:

- (315 million people in the US) x (90 percent people have a cell phone) x (50 percent will be buying a new phone this year) = 142 million

The number of people that will buy the iPhone each year:

- (142 million people that will be buying a new phone this year) x (60 percent will get a smartphone) x (40 percent of the smartphone buyers will buy an iPhone) = 34 million

To conclude, 34 million iPhones are sold in the US each year.

Comments: The candidate's assumptions, methodology and calculations are reasonable. However, his delivery is a bit abrupt. He rattles off assumptions without giving us the big picture. Then the numbers are just crunched at the end. It would have been easier to follow if the candidate multiplied the numbers as he was uncovering his assumptions.

Estimate how much it costs to run Flickr for a 20 GB user.

CANDIDATE: Just a quick clarification, when you say 20 GB user, are you saying that the user is using 20 GB of storage, or they bought a plan, which allows them up to 20 GB storage?

INTERVIEWER: The latter.

CANDIDATE: I assume you want me to calculate costs of actual usage. That is, if they signed up for a 20 GB plan, and they use something less than 20 GB. That's the number you want?

INTERVIEWER: Yes.

CANDIDATE: And you want me to estimate costs per year or per month?

INTERVIEWER: Per month.

CANDIDATE: Okay. Let's say that each Flickr user uploads 10 pictures per week.

Each picture is roughly 5 MB in size.

Multiply 10 by 5 MB each. That's 50 MB each week. That's about 2.5 GB of storage for the year. But what we really need is the average cost at any given point in the year. So let's just take the mid-point, and the average user, in its first year has about 1.25 GB.

Let's talk about storage costs. I'll estimate storage costs to be 10 cents per GB per month. That's roughly how much Amazon S3 charges for storage. We're storing 1.25 GB per user, so multiply that with $.10 per GB/mo. gives us 12.5 cents per month. Per year, that's $1.50 per user.

From a bandwidth perspective, we usually show the optimized version of the photo. Let's assume optimization can reduce file sizes by 40 percent. So rather than see the full 5 MB, let's say the user sees a 2MB version.

Assume each picture gets viewed on average 10 times per month. So that's 10 x 2 MB each, so 20 MB gets transferred.

We assumed that the user uploads 10 pictures per week. That's 520 photos per year. Let's take the midpoint again, and we get 260 photos. So that's 5.2 GB per month.

Let's say the bandwidth costs are 12 cents per GB per month. If we round our 5.2 GB to 5 GB, we get 60 cents per month per user.

Comments: The flow, calculations and clarification questions are good. There are several numbers that are being crunched, and the interviewer could get lost. The candidate could improve comprehension by drawing his approach on the whiteboard and doing the calculations on the whiteboard instead of rattling off numbers and using his notepad for a math scratch pad.

How many elevators do you need for a 50-story building?

CANDIDATE: You just care about my thought process for this question, right?

INTERVIEWER: Your thought process is important, but I also want you to come up with an actual number.

CANDIDATE: Okay. Give me a moment to collect my thoughts.

Candidate pauses for 30 seconds

CANDIDATE: I'm going to evaluate the number of elevators we need based on how many passengers we need to transport.

To start, I'll estimate how many people use the elevators and how long they're willing to wait. In the elevator industry, it's assumed that people are willing to wait 20 seconds for an elevator. It's also important to know how many people enter the building during peak times. I forgot to ask: is this building for office, retail, or residential use?

INTERVIEWER: This is an office building.

CANDIDATE: If the first part was all about elevator demand, this second part is about elevator capacity. I'd like to estimate:

- How many people can fit an elevator?
- What's the elevator's average speed?
- How long does an elevator stay open before closing and resuming travel?

It may also be important to know whether there are alternative transportation methods such as stairs or escalators. For the sake of simplicity, we'll set that aside.

Let's assume this is a 50 story office building and that each floor contains 120 employees. In total, that's 6,000 people in a 50 story office building.

People get to work between 8 a.m. and 9 a.m. The 6,000 people arrive uniformly during this 60 min. duration. That's 100 people per minute.

We want people to wait no more than 20 seconds per elevator. 33 people, on average, wait 20 seconds.

To determine how many elevators are needed to transport 33 people once every 20 seconds, we need to determine the effective throughput of an elevator.

Let's assume there are 12 feet per floor and the elevator travels 20 feet per second. Let's also assume that in a 50 story building, the elevator stops 12 times on its way up, and each stop takes about 20 seconds.

Let's calculate the numbers. There are 600 feet in this building. At 20 feet per second, it takes 30 seconds to get to the top. However, there are 12 stops on the way up, so that takes 240 seconds. On average, it takes 270 seconds to go up. Let's say it takes half the time to make it's way down in the morning or 135 seconds. In total that's 6.75 minutes to go up and down.

Let's say each elevator can contain 10 people. It would take 3.3 elevators to transport the first batch of waiting passengers. Since 6.75 minutes will have elapsed before those first set of 3.3 elevators make its way back, you'll need an additional 67 elevators to service them all.

Just to gut check my solution, Seattle's Columbia Tower has 83 floors, and they have 46 elevators.

Comments: Candidate asked some good clarifying questions and demonstrated customer empathy. Nice approach of evaluating demand first, then capacity. A potential follow-up question is discussing elevator algorithms to service incoming requests, which is covered later in the book.

Chapter 9 Getting Analytical: Pricing

Pricing interview questions determine whether candidates can diagnose an ambiguous situation, formulate a methodical way of tackling it and make a hard decision that could make or break an organization.

How to Approach a Pricing Problem

When it comes to pricing, the most important number to know is the customer's willingness to pay. For products that are creating brand new categories, this is the price of building a particular product from scratch. For products that compete in existing categories, this is the competitors' price plus an additional accessories or customizations necessary to achieve parity with the competition.

In the real world, the best way to finalize price is to try different price points. Out of all retailers, Amazon is known to be most aggressive in varying its price over time, finding the optimal balance between price and volume.

What is you can't run real-time price experiments like Amazon? You can survey customers instead. But note that surveys can lead to overly optimistic predictions on price points and volume. You'll have to take that data and adjust accordingly to have a more accurate assessment.

Practice Questions

1. How would you price the Kindle Fire HD?
2. Assume you are the new product manager in our Amazon Prime business and are deciding pricing. The vice president would like to lower the price from $79.99 per year to $69.99 per year. Making your own assumptions, develop the financial projections for this decision.

Answers

How would you price the Kindle Fire HD?

CANDIDATE: My understanding is that Kindle Fire HD is a 7-inch tablet with an HD display. I'm not familiar with the tablet market. Do I mind if ask you a few questions?

INTERVIEWER: Sure, go ahead.

CANDIDATE: Who are its main competitors?

INTERVIEWER: The main competitors are the iPad Mini, Samsung Galaxy Tab, and Google's Nexus 7.

CANDIDATE: How much do those retail for?

INTERVIEWER: The iPad Mini retails for $329 while the Galaxy Tab and Nexus 7 sell for $199.

CANDIDATE: What makes Kindle Fire HD standout from its competition?

INTERVIEWER: Kindle Fire HD has a higher resolution than the Galaxy Tab and iPad Mini.

My last question: How much does it cost to make a Kindle Fire HD?

I can't release internal data. However, a market research firm, iSuppli, disassembled a Kindle Fire HD and publicly estimated that each Kindle Fire HD costs $174 to make.

CANDIDATE: Thanks for the background information. There are three different ways we can look at pricing.

Candidate writes on the board

- *Customer's willingness to pay*

- *Competitive pricing*
- *Cost-based pricing*

CANDIDATE: First, I'd think about the customer. If they didn't have the product, what would they do instead? How much they would pay for an alternative or substitute product? Negotiators call this the BATNA or the best alternative to a negotiated agreement. Here, I'll call it the customer's willingness to pay for the product. It represents the maximum a customer would pay for the product.

In this case, if a customer couldn't buy a Kindle Fire HD, the best alternative device is the Nexus 7. It has specifications, especially screen resolution, that's most similar to the Fire HD. The Nexus 7 costs $199, so that likely is the most we could charge for the Kindle Fire HD.

Next, we look at Kindle Fire HD's unit cost of $174. We can add an absolute or relative markup to the unit's final price. Knowing how strategic the Fire HD is to selling additional digital content, it's possible that Amazon could pursue the "razor and razor blade" strategy. That is, sell the Kindle Fire HD at, or below, cost, and make its profits on future digital content sales. Given this, let's say the pricing lower bound could be $174.

Then, we compare prices with what's already on the market. The Nexus 7 and the Galaxy Tab are selling for $199.

Finally, we should evaluate supply and demand. Limited supply and high demand might merit a higher price point while the inverse might merit the reverse. To build a demand curve, we can test different price points. From that data, we can extrapolate the right price to maximize overall product profits.

INTERVIEWER: So what's your recommendation?

CANDIDATE: Given the urgency, there's no time to experiment and derive a supply and demand curve. Based on the discussion, we've got a tight pricing bound from $174 to $199. I would recommend the low end of the pricing spectrum, $174. Amazon needs to protect its core business of selling books, music, and movies. In the digital world, iTunes and Google Play can sell books. By ceding control of the platform, the tablet, Amazon will find it hard to compete. It's more important that Amazon wins market share now and create a strong distribution footprint of tablets. Using the Kindle Fire HD as a loss leader, Amazon can generate profits on future sales of digital content.

Comments: Candidate used an easy-to-follow pricing framework. The interviewer perceived the candidate to be an expert. It's not feasible to build supply and demand curves in the interview, but the acknowledgment is important. It was also good that the candidate recommended a specific price. Other candidates may have fallen short and refused to commit. It may come as a surprise that the candidate can ask for so much background information. But he must because he doesn't know much about the tablet market or the price points. It would be lethal to answer based on assumptions and be criticized for a wrong detail.

Assume you are the new product manager in our Amazon Prime business and are deciding pricing. The vice president would like to lower the price from $79.99 per year to $69.99 per year. Making your own assumptions, develop the financial projections for this decision.

CANDIDATE: With lower prices, customer demand will increase. The new Prime customers might also purchase more things. However, increased demand will reduce membership revenues from existing Prime customers and increase shipping costs for existing non-Prime customers. Let's assume there are 5 million Prime customers.

Existing Prime customers

With a $10 price reduction that reduces annual revenues by $50 million.

New Prime customers

We need to estimate how many new Prime customers will be gained from the changes. Finally, let's consider additional revenue from the membership, along with incremental sales.

Let's say Prime membership jumps 20 percent due to the price cut. That's an additional 1 million Prime customers. The incremental membership revenue is roughly $70 million. Average shipping costs per customer is around $40 per year. Let's say that moving these customers into Prime increases shipping costs by $20 per year per new Prime customer. That's an additional $20MM cost.

Lastly, we can anticipate more frequent purchases due to free 2-day shipping. Let's say there's an additional $40 worth of purchases per new Prime customer per year. Amazon's gross margins are 25%, so that's an extra $10 per year per new Prime customer.

To recap on the net annual impact:

Existing Prime customers

-$10 million net

New Prime customers

+$60 million net = +$70 million member revenue -$20 million incremental shipping costs + $10 million incremental gross margin

INTERVIEWER: So what's the overall change in revenue, and what's your recommendation?

CANDIDATE: Overall, we're looking at a $50 million annual increase from reducing price from $10. I recommend we reduce price.

Comments: Candidate covered all the primary dimensions: increases in revenue and costs, as well as impact with respect to new and existing customers. Candidate had to make a lot of assumptions, but that's typical as many interviewers are tight-lipped on details and assumptions.

Chapter 10 Getting Analytic

The Internet made it simple to do A/B testing, allo[...]
managers to evaluate a feature with a subset of use[...]
may be received by all users. Now, most Agile pro[...]
processes rely on A/B experimentation instead of crude human
judgment to make decisions. (For quick background, Agile product
development emphasizes iterative development rather than
determining requirements upfront and building the product in a single,
final release.) Product managers are leading the charge with A/B
testing: developing new features and hypotheses on what will improve
product performance, evaluating test results, and making ship or no-
ship decisions on new releases.

The metrics interview reflects this new reality. Interviewers routinely
ask individuals what metrics they would evaluate to understand success
of a product, how they would interpret test results and what actions
they would take based on the data.

The interviewer is assessing whether the candidate understands metrics
that relate to the overall business goal and whether they can drive the
A/B testing process.

How to Approach Metrics Questions

When asked to define metrics for a product, keep AARM Metrics™ in
mind.

What are the AARM Metrics™?

A cquisition

A ctivation

R etention

M onetization

...on is all about signing up customers to a service. The bar for ...ng up for a service has gotten lower and lower, thanks to the ...pularity of free signup and pay later "freemium" models. The typical metric to track here is lazy registrations.

Activation is getting users that have completed a lazy registration to fully register. For a social networking site like Google+, this may include uploading a photo or completing their profile page.

Retention is getting users to use the service often and behave in a way that help the user or the business. Key metrics include adding more information to their profile page, checking the news feed frequently, or inviting friends to try the service.

Monetization is collecting revenue from users. It could include the number of people who are paying for the service or the average revenue per user (ARPU).

What are the Three Loops™?

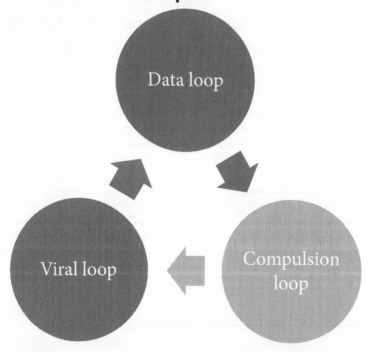

My favorite visual to remind me of key retention metrics is this visual, which I call the Three Loops™. The first loop is the data loop, or adding more information. For instance, adding a photo or a list of favorite movies is contributing to Facebook's data loop.

The second loop is the compulsion loop. This is about checking an application frequently. For example, Zynga's mobile games ask users to check-in throughout the day to see how their farm has grown or to see how many new tokens they've generated.

The last loop is the viral loop. This is about inviting friends to try the service. For example, LinkedIn encourages users to invite more connections. Adding connections makes LinkedIn more valuable to the users; it'll allow them to contact more people and see more profile information. And LinkedIn is thrilled that users will serve as ambassadors for their service, which would reduce their customer acquisition costs.

The Three Loops™ also point out how each loop reinforces the other. As a single user adds more personal information to a service, it compels their friends to check the service more often. When the friends see the new information, the friends find the service more valuable, pushing them to invite more contacts. And when new people join the service, they'll add more data, starting the cycle anew.

Tip: Making Decisions from A/B Test Results

Ideally, we would run A/B test experiments for win-win situations. For example, it would be amazing if a new feature was found to increase revenue by 5 percent and seven-day logins by 3 percent. However, the real world often requires us to make win-lose tradeoffs. For instance, a particular feature could increase revenue 5 percent, but 30-day logins decrease by 3 percent. What should a product manager do?

When faced with this dilemma, make the decision that's in-line with the corporate strategic goal. Ask the interviewer. What's the current objective? If the owner is desperate to meet a quarterly profit goal, choose the feature that maximizes revenue at the expense of engagement. If engagement's the goal, choose that over maximizing revenue.

Practice Question

1. What metrics will you look at to evaluate success of a product?
2.   Suggest a killer feature to improve LinkedIn? And what metrics would you track to determine success?
3.   What feature would you build to improve Google+? And what metrics would you track to determine success?

Answers

What metrics will you look at to evaluate success of a product?

INTERVIEWER: LinkedIn is testing a new feature: asking a new user to upload their profile photo during the signup phase. Currently, a new user is asked to upload a profile photo after the sign-up process. What metrics will you look at to evaluate success of a product?

CANDIDATE: Give me a moment to collect my thoughts.

Candidate writes the following on the whiteboard

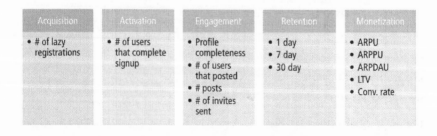

Acquisition	Activation	Engagement	Retention	Monetization
• # of lazy registrations	• # of users that complete signup	• Profile completeness • # of users that posted • # posts • # of invites sent	• 1 day • 7 day • 30 day	• ARPU • ARPPU • ARPDAU • LTV • Conv. rate

CANDIDATE: Here are the metrics that I would consider: acquisition, activation, engagement, retention, and monetization.

For acquisition, we might track the number of lazy registrations.

For activation, we might look at the number of people that complete the entire signup process.

For engagement, we might look at a variety of metrics including profile completeness, the number of users that posted, the number of posts they make, and the number of invites sent.

For retention, I'd look at how often they return to our site within single-, 7- and 30-day windows.

Lastly, for monetization, I'd consider a few different metrics including:

- Average revenue per user (ARPU)
- Average revenue per paying user (ARPPU)
- Average revenue per daily active user (ARPDAU)
- Lifetime value (LTV)
- Conversion rate

Candidate crosses out Acquisition and Monetization boxes

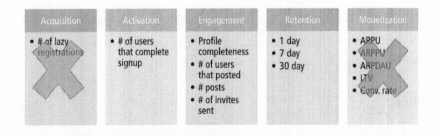

CANDIDATE: To help us maintain focus, we don't need to track the number of lazy registrations because this feature change doesn't affect the lazy registration process. And for similar reasons, we don't need to worry about monetization metrics.

INTERVIEWER: Okay, let's continue to the next step: you run the upload profile feature in signup flow feature for a two-week A/B test. Here are the results:

	Lift	P-Value
Number of users completing signup	-13.21 percent	0.02
Profile completeness	+1.65 percent	0.01
Number of users the posted	+2.11 percent	0.05
Number of posts	+4.85 percent	0.01
Number of invites sent	+2.36 percent	0.02
1 day retention	+2.12 percent	0.07
7 day retention	+1.08 percent	0.20
30 day retention	N/A	N/A

INTERVIEWER: Tell me what's going on.

CANDIDATE: On the one hand, engagement has gone up significantly. Increases in the number of posts and invites sent are remarkable. The number of users posting and 7 day retention is not bad either.

However, there's a double-digit drop in the number of users completing signup.

This is a tough call. This feels a bit one step forward and one step back. However, I think we're getting a good tradeoff here. That is, what's the point of getting more users (that complete the signup) if they're not going to use the product down the road? Having more engaged users is worth it in my opinion.

INTERVIEWER: One last question: why did we show the p-value column?

CANDIDATE: P-value is a measure of whether our results are statistically valid. That is, with a sufficient p-value, we know that our results can't be explained by something other than the feature changed specified in the A/B test. Typically, I am comfortable accept data with a p-value less than .05.

Comments: The candidate did a good job articulating metrics, evaluating the data and explaining the concept of p-values. This type of question is more likely for an online business, where they do weekly A/B testing. The interviewer is testing whether you can identify the right metrics, evaluate test results appropriately and make reasonable decisions from the data.

Notice how the candidate didn't strictly follow the AARM Method™. That's okay. The goal of frameworks is to serve as a mental checklist for a complete response, not to recite it verbatim at the interview. Adapt the framework as you see fit.

Suggest a killer feature to improve LinkedIn? And what metrics would you track to determine success?

CANDIDATE: There are a lot of different reasons why people use LinkedIn. Professionals could be looking for jobs or career development opportunities. Recruiters could be looking for new candidates. Sales people could be looking for new contacts.

For me, the persona that resonates most is the professional. I'm always searching for conferences and courses focused on professional development. That's the scenario I'd like to explore.

INTERVIEWER: Go ahead.

CANDIDATE: When I think about the conference scenario, I think of three use cases:

1. As a potential conference attendee, I want to find new conferences so that I can attend.

2. As a conference attendee, I'd like to see who else is attending the conference, so that I can keep a list of people to network before, during, and after.

3. As a conference attendee, I'd like to have the conference materials easily accessible for reference.

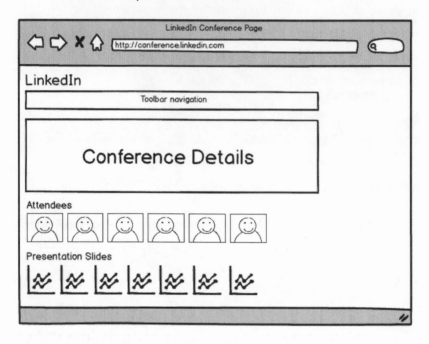

So here's my solution: a conference page hosted on LinkedIn. It would have conference details, such as event name, date, location, cost, and links to conference agenda.

Right below it would be registered attendees. Users can click to contact via LinkedIn's messaging system. And below that would be links to pre and post conference slide material.

LinkedIn's revenue opportunities with this new conference page could include:

- Conference organizers pay monthly subscription fees
- Get revenue share on all conference fees
- Collect a small transaction fee on all registrations

INTERVIEWER: Interesting. Let's talk about getting ⬛ data. How would you do it?

CANDIDATE: Three ideas come to mind:

1. Conference organizers can post details manually.
2. Build a crawler to index the web and parse conference data.
3. Define a conference data format and have conference organizers upload the data to LinkedIn, either in a text file or a server-to-server API call.

INTERVIEWER: How would you determine if this new feature is successful?

CANDIDATE: There are a couple of metrics I would consider:

- **Acquisition.** How many conference organizers have we signed up for the service? This measure tells us whether or not the feature is compelling is worth spending their time on.
- **Engagement.** Of the conference organizers who have signed up, how many conference pages have they created? How often? And for the conference attendees, how often do they visit the site? What kind of positive behaviors have they undertaken, whether it's contacting or connecting with other conference attendees? Or downloading presentation materials? We want the feature to add value to both organizers and attendees.
- **Monetization.** Lastly, how much money are we making? I wouldn't want us to waste time working on something that's not contributing either short or long term revenue potential.

Comments: Candidate does a good job picking a single persona and articulating use cases. The idea is solid and not something LinkedIn offers today. From an implementation perspective, the biggest

ınd the candidate has three alternative
ement, the candidate could have
of each solution. In the metrics section,
od ideas. However, we also see that his
over the place. Had he clearly specified the
ure at the beginning of the interview, he
likeı, more specific on his choice of metrics.

What feature would you build to improve Google+? And what metrics would you track to determine success?

CANDIDATE: Google+ is the number two social network, after Facebook. It has over 500 million users. Google+'s biggest problem: people don't use the service. The signup numbers show that there isn't an awareness problem. It's an interest problem. It's like a nightclub. Google+ users assume that there's nothing interesting going on in the Google+ news feed.

I have an interesting insight that could help us address this engagement problem. A recent research study that says social network users engage most with photos, followed by videos, shared links and text updates.

INTERVIEWER: How do you define engagement?

CANDIDATE: In this study, engagement is defined by likes, comments, and views – on a photo, video, etc.

INTERVIEWER: I see.

CANDIDATE: The study got me thinking of my own news feed: I don't have pets, but many of my friends have pets. I love seeing pictures of my friends' pets. And I imagine my friends love sharing pet photos.

INTERVIEWER: Ok, it sounds like an opportunity. What do you next?

CANDIDATE: When I put myself in a pet owner's shoes, here are the first three scenarios that come to mind:

1. As a pet owner, I want to create a pet page so that friends and other acquaintances can follow the pets' activity, not the owner's activity.
2. As a pet owner, I want to easily share pet photos and videos to my pet's personal pet page, so that it doesn't take too much time.
3. As a pet owner, I want to share experiences from the pet's perspective so that I get more enjoyment from having a pet.

INTERVIEWER: All three sound interesting. Given our limited time, which one did you want to focus on?

CANDIDATE: The first two make a lot of sense. But I think we can come up with some creative things for the 3rd use case.

INTERIVEWER: Okay.

CANDIDATE: I have three potential solutions on how we can share the pet's perspective.

1. **Add a Google Glass headset to the pet**. Take photos or videos at set intervals. Automatically upload photos to the pet's page. The benefit is to get the pet's point of view, while making it seamless to share with friends and followers.
2. **FitBit for dogs**. FitBit is a device that tracks a human's physical activity. It can report number of steps walked and quality of sleep. This is primarily for health-conscious owners. They want to determine if the pet is getting proper amount of exercise. This information can also be shared on a pet's social network feed.

This scarf makes my eyez sparkle.

JELLUS???

3. **Cheezburger + Dog FitBit**. Cheezburger is a humor website known for appending funny captions to pet photos. My proposed idea is to automatically post humorous pet sayings to a social network, based on the dog's tracked physical activity via a FitBit-like device.

INTERVIEWER: Creative. Let's talk about the Cheezburger-esque idea. What are the top features?

CANDIDATE: Off the top of my head, there are a couple of features & technologies to enable this:

1. FitBit-like device to track physical activity
2. A rules engine or artificial intelligence to map physical activities to humorous sayings
3. A service that posts humorous sayings to a social network

INTERVIEWER: Of the three features you suggested, which one would be the most difficult to implement?

I'm not an expert in FitBit devices or social network technology. But since both product categories exist for humans, I feel that it's doable for pets.

Thus, the biggest challenge is the rules engine. I'm not aware of a rules engine that can map a dog's, or even a human's, physical activity to humorous sayings.

INTERVIEWER: Help me understand. What do you mean by humorous sayings?

CANDIDATE: Let's say it's late Sunday morning. The dog is frantically pacing the garage for 5-10 minutes, followed by 15 minutes of howling. The dog owners can indicate that they are doing their weekly Costco shopping trip and that the pet is having some separation anxiety. This physical activity could be mapped to a funny saying such as "Mom and Dad are out for Costco shopping. Better bring back a hot dog; otherwise, I'm going to mess up their favorite recliner real bad."

INTERVIEWER: Got it.

CANDIDATE: It would likely require some detailed manual coding to map physical and geographic activity to a particular scenario. To start, we do simple mappings. For example, if a pet is running 2 miles at 10 miles an hour, we can easily decode that situation as going for a run.

INTERVIEWER: Let's say you've got V1 built. What are the top three metrics to evaluate success?

CANDIDATE: There are three metrics I would consider purchases, friend engagement, and usage.

Purchases are important because it helps us evaluate whether or not the value proposition is resonating with the customer. I love the idea, but my personal opinion is not a good proxy for the overall market.

Friend engagement is critical because that's what we're ultimately shooting for: more news feed updates to drive more Google+ usage. The key question is: do people literally like the news feed posts from our Cheezburger + Dog FitBit idea? Do we get a lot of comments? Do people who engage with these news posts visit Google+ more often for longer durations?

Lastly, usage is essential. I wonder if this is something that pet owners will use once in a while, or if they will have it on for 24/7. If we prove that this device will drive Google+ usage, we want the device to be as often as possible, driving more Google+ updates.

INTERVIEWER: What per user usage metrics would you track?

CANDIDATE: I'd choose changes in 30-day actives as well as sessions per day.

Comments: Candidate does a good job using the CIRCLES Method™ design and AARM Method™ metrics framework, without sounding mechanical. In addition to leading a logical discussion, the user differentiates himself from others with his creativity. With the Cheezburger + Dogs FitBit solution, he took three different parts and combined it into a unique whole. We can infer that the candidate utilized an attribute-based brainstorming to quickly come up with this idea.

The initial unique insight sets up the discussion nicely along with the quick focus to a particular persona, the pet owner.

Chapter 11 Strategizing: Tradeoffs

When it comes to strategy, the most prevalent and satisfying analysis tool is pro/con analysis. As the name implies, it's satisfying because it feels objective. How can something not be objective if you evaluate both the positives and negatives? It also feels complete. If one were to evaluate the pros and cons of an idea, across three to five different dimensions, this analysis would easily consume two to four minutes.

Practice Questions

1. Amazon launched display advertisements on its web page, and it was a highly controversial decision within the company. Pick either the pro or con side of the argument and explain your position for or against including ads on the site.
2. Now tell me why display advertising is a bad decision.

Answers

Amazon launched display advertisements on its web page, and it was a highly controversial decision within the company. Pick either the pro or con side of the argument and explain your position for or against including ads on the site.

CANDIDATE: Give me a moment to think about this.

Candidate takes 60 seconds.

CANDIDATE: Launching Amazon display advertisements is a good decision and there are two reasons why:

It helps customer experience. Advertisements can minimize negative customer experiences and possibly enhance a positive customer experience. Let's say a customer was intent on buying a product, but Amazon is out of stock. The customer was going to leave the site

135

anyway. Amazon can direct the consumer to a competitor that does have the product, enhancing the customer experience. Alternatively, advertising can highlight special offers, enhancing the Amazon shopping experience.

It provides additional revenue. Advertisers will pay Amazon to achieve the advertiser's business goals. For instance, manufacturers might want to increase awareness, increase upsell, or shift share away from competitor's products.

There's even an opportunity to sell ads to Amazon's competitors. Amazon's competitors may be too happy to meet an Amazon customer's unmet purchase needs.

The latter case may feel bizarre, but there is a revenue opportunity, along with an opportunity for improved customer satisfaction. This revenue can be used to further invest in the Amazon customer experience.

Comments: The interviewer is testing the candidate's ability to make a proposal and back it with evidence. The key is to be precise and specific, avoiding the corporate jargon and nonsense words that cloud most corporate communications. Stay factual, or at least logical, because subjective statements, invite skepticism particularly if they're not backed with evidence. Having numbers and hard data always helps. Also, be decisive and have hard conviction behind a single position. The interviewer will note candidates who refuse to commit one way or the other.

Now tell me why display advertising is a bad decision.

CANDIDATE: Launching display advertisements on Amazon are a bad decision, and here's why:

Distracts customers from purchasing products

Ads can clutter the customer experience. For example, it may be harder for the customer to find what they want. In the short-term, it could lead to increased bounce rates, more abandoned shopping carts and reduced conversions. In the long-term, it could lead to fewer repeat visits as customers search for shopping alternatives that are less cluttered and frustrating.

Create a negative brand perception

Over time, customers could notice that Amazon repeatedly refers customers to other retailers. Rather than come to Amazon as their first shopping destination, they may choose to go to those retailers first. This will give the competitor an opportunity to establish their reputation as the first place to find & research products they need.

Comments: This is a common follow-up question to the previous question. The interviewer is seeing how quickly a candidate can abandon your previous position, take a new position and identify the right arguments for the opposing view. It's testing whether a candidate can see both sides of the issue, adapt to change and leave behind a preconceived notion of what should have been done.

Chapter 12 Strategizing: New Market entry

How to Approach Strategy Questions on New Market Entry

To answer interview questions on entering new markets, run through the following checklist during your discussion. Your checklist offers tangible criteria for which the interviewer can agree or disagree with your assessment. The checklist makes sure that nothing is left off of your analysis.

New Market Entry Checklist

Market characteristics

- Market size
- Market growth
- Profit margins
- Market trends, including changing customer preferences and regulatory changes

Competitive environment

- Number of competitors
- Competitor's resources, including financial, employees, and partner ecosystem
- Competitor's unique competencies, including differentiated products, access to distribution channels

Company fit

- Expertise
- Economies of scale
- Access to distribution channels

- Good relationships with suppliers

  Related to existing brand promise

Practice Questions

1. You have a choice between selling a new oven or an oven mitt. Which one do you choose and why?

2. An aspiring Amazon product manager proposes to Jeff Bezos that Amazon should sell groceries from neighborhood markets. What are the pros and cons of this idea?

Answers

Start a new category, division, or international market for Amazon. Which one did you choose and why?

CANDIDATE: I would start a dollar store category for Amazon. It's a good fit for the following reasons:

Growing market	5-7 percent annual growth
Good gross margins	30-40 percent vs. Amazon's 20-28 percent
Attractive customer segment	22 percent of dollar store customers make $70k+ per year
Consistent w/ strategy	Dollar store improves product selection
Low barriers to entry	Amazon likely has relationships with dollar item manufacturers already
Synergies	Physical products can utilize Amazon's superior fulfillment capabilities
Credible differentiation	Dollar store value without the driving and the slimy store experience

Today, I see Amazon dabbling with dollar store items. Sometimes, there are some dollar items available for sale, but definitely not the breadth that I'd see at a brick and mortar dollar store. Other times, I would see dollar store items such as baking soda, get marked up 400 percent by Amazon's marketplace vendors.

With the new add on program, Amazon clearly recognizes that selling low-priced items can be profitable; they just can't be profitable (or provide sufficient customer value) when they're being sold and shipped on its own.

The dollar store would work under the "fill your bag" principle. That is, buy enough $1 items to fill a minimum quantity, and you'll get Amazon's free super saver shipping. By aggregating several $1 items in a single shipment, Amazon can make these dollar items profitable.

Comments: This is a very difficult question because Amazon carries almost every physical good. Here's a list of physical goods not currently sold by Amazon:

- **Pets**
- **Guns**
- **Cars**
- **Marijuana**
- **Prescription drugs**

The physical goods above have strict regulations. And cars are too bulky to use Amazon's current fulfillment infrastructure.

A new international market can be a reasonable answer. However, it requires detailed international knowledge to be credible. Good products to choose leverage Amazon's strengths including their:

- **Brand**
- **Distribution footprint**

- Merchandising platform
- Fulfillment infrastructure
- Customer service

You have a choice between selling a new oven or an oven mitt. Which one do you choose and why?

CANDIDATE: My understanding of the scenario is that I'm an Amazon category manager, responsible for the kitchen category. I have to choose which new product to carry—a new oven or oven mitt.

INTERVIEWER: Yes, that's correct. You have to make the tough decision of choosing just one.

CANDIDATE: Let me walk you through how I would frame the issue and then dive into the details.

INTERVIEWER: Sounds good.

CANDIDATE: So there are three criteria I think about when stocking a new product.

Candidate writes the following on the whiteboard:

- *Profitability*
- *Customer satisfaction*
- *Product assortment*

CANDIDATE: To begin, profitability is straightforward. Usually it doesn't make sense to go through the effort, cost, and time to stock a product if we're not going to make money off of it.

Secondly, customer satisfaction is important for two reasons. The first is that we want customers to have a good experience. Customers will be disappointed if they can't find a product. This affects net promoter customer satisfaction metric.

Moreover, Amazon should recommend high quality products. Amazon wouldn't want to endorse, let alone carry, products that either don't work as advertised or don't provide reasonable value to customers.

Third, product assortment is crucial, especially as it relates to corporate strategy and branding. Amazon's value proposition is product assortment. Amazon started by promoting itself as the world's largest bookstore and now, rightfully so, the world's largest store, period.

If customers expect Amazon to stock a particular item and that item weren't available, Amazon's brand equity would be damaged. It would affect customers' desire to come back in the future as well as their willingness to recommend Amazon to friends. I know Amazon doesn't spend a lot on traditional marketing, choosing instead to let consumer experience speak for itself; so a negative customer experience would be detrimental.

Is there anything missing from my decision-making framework?

INTERVIEWER: I can't think of anything else from the top of my head.

Candidate writes on the whiteboard:

	Oven	Oven Mitt
Annual profit contribution	$XX million	$YY million
Increase in customer satisfaction	Carrying the oven <increases / decreases> cust. sat. because _____	Carrying the oven mitt <increases / decreases> cust. sat. because _____
Improvement in product assortment	Carrying the oven <increases / decreases> prod. asst. because _____	Carrying the oven <increases / decreases> prod. asst. because _____

CANDIDATE: I would assess each product in order.

INTERVIEWER: Okay, I like that approach. Let's start with the qualitative ones first—customer satisfaction and product assortment.

CANDIDATE: Okay. Does Amazon carry any ovens today?

INTERVIEWER: No. We carry small toasters, but we do not carry large kitchen ovens. Why do you think that is?

CANDIDATE: My hypothesis is that consumers aren't comfortable buying large appliances online. They are used to going to Sears, Best Buy, and Home Depot to buy appliances in person. However, I do think the world is changing. I bought a kitchen oven 3 months ago, and I bought it from Best Buy's website after seeing listed for more at Home Depot.

INTERVIEWER: Ah, showrooming.

CANDIDATE: Yes.

INTERVIEWER: Aside from consumer behavior, why else would Amazon not carry kitchen ovens?

Candidate thinks for a moment.

CANDIDATE: I can come up with two more reasons why Amazon doesn't carry kitchen ovens today. First, because of its bulky nature, a kitchen oven isn't easy to deliver, especially in Amazon's highly optimized fulfillment operation that had its roots in delivering more manageable items, such as books, DVDs, and movies.

INTERVIEWER: Correct. What else?

CANDIDATE: Amazon might also not sell ovens because that is more a solution-sell, not a product-sell.

INTERVIEWER: Sounds like jargon to me. What does "solution-sell" mean?

CANDIDATE: Well, the customer is not just buying an oven; he wants a working oven. To sell a working oven, Amazon would also have to provide installation services as part of the sell. Home Depot and Best Buy have developed relationships with local service providers who can not only deliver kitchen ovens, but have the expertise to install them, too. Amazon would have to develop those business relationships on a nationwide scale.

INTERVIEWER: Based on your findings, what would you put in the customer satisfaction section of your scorecard, for the new oven?

CANDIDATE: I would put "decrease" customer satisfaction. We could carry ovens and make them available for sale. However, we wouldn't be able to fulfill customers in the quick manner that they expect from Amazon. Also, we'd have a hard time offering the services that go along with the big appliance purchase from Day 1.

INTERVIEWER: Sounds good. We're running short on time. I want us to cover one last thing before we move onto the next question.

CANDIDATE: Sure.

INTERVIEWER: I'd like you to calculate the expected profits from carrying the oven mitt.

CANDIDATE: You want an actual number estimate?

INTERVIEWER: Yes.

CANDIDATE: And when you say profits, do you mean annual or lifetime?

INTERVIEWER: Annual.

CANDIDATE: I'll talk about my approach and then we'll go into some back-of-the-envelope calculations. I'll start off with looking at the potential customer base, the likelihood of purchasing an oven mitt at Amazon, the frequency of purchase, and the propensity to purchase a particular model. And of course, I'll also factor in the profit margin.

INTERVIEWER: Sounds good.

CANDIDATE: Last time I checked there are 315 million people in the US. I'm going to guess there are roughly 2.5 people per household. To save time, we'll round the numbers to 300 million and three, respectively. This will give us 100 million households.

Most households need one oven mitt. There are some that need more than one, but let's say one is sufficient.

For this year, there are two customer segments that would be interested in oven mitts. The first customer segment is households that have never owned an oven mitt. The second customer segment is households that want to replace an oven mitt.

Let's start with the first segment. Those who are starting households are usually new college grads. If we assume a uniform distribution along with a 70-year life expectancy, we'll get:

Candidate writes down:

300 million people / 70 year life expectancy = 4.3 million new people starting a household each year

CANDIDATE: Of those 4.3 million people, not everyone will get an oven mitt. Some think they need it, some don't. Some have one from mom and dad. What's a reasonable assumption for percentage of new grads that need an oven mitt?

INTERVIEWER: Go with 60.

Candidate writes down:

4.3MM * 60% = 2.6 million

CANDIDATE: Okay, that's 2.6 million people who are going to buy the oven mitt.

Next calculation: what percent buy from Amazon? What do you think is Amazon's market share of oven mitt purchases?

INTERVIEWER: What do you think it is?

CANDIDATE: It seems that most people buy housewares from Target and other big box retailers, so I'd say it's less than 5 percent. However, younger people like buying through Amazon, especially with free shipping and Prime; so I'd go with a higher number, like 15 percent.

INTERVIEWER: Sure.

Candidate writes down:

2.6 million * 15 percent = 390k

CANDIDATE: Of those 390 thousand people, I'll assume they only need one oven mitt. For these folks, how many would buy this particular oven mitt? Is there anything special about the oven mitt that leads us to believe that it would get a disproportionate number of sales?

INTERVIEWER: Initial tests show that it outsells the average oven mitt by 3:1.

CANDIDATE: How many oven mitts do you carry?

INTERVIEWER: 2,000.

Candidate writes down:

390k / 2k = 195 units per average mitt

195 avg. units * 3 = 585 units sold for this mitt, per year

CANDIDATE: So we're expected to sell 585 mitts this year. What's the unit contribution for each mitt?

INTERVIEWER: $4.

Candidate writes down:

585 units per year * $4 = $2,340 annual profits

CANDIDATE: From a profit perspective, carrying this mitt will bring us $2,340 in annual profits.

INTERVIEWER: We're running out of time. Based on what you know, does it make sense to carry the oven mitt?

CANDIDATE: Amazon already carries 2,000 mitts, so it's hard to argue that customers are unsatisfied with the current set of choices or find the product selection lacking.

The $2,340 in annual profits is nice, but there may be some cannibalization. Cannibalization concerns aside, along with any upsell/cross-sell considerations, I would only go for the $2,340 in annual profits if it doesn't require any additional work, such as starting a new vendor relationship.

Comments: The candidate showed a lot of dexterity in this problem. The interviewer wanted to evaluate the candidate's ability to tackling a strategic issue, and it ended with detailed calculations on profit potential. Candidate showed good stamina and did an excellent job all around.

An aspiring Amazon product manager proposes to Jeff Bezos that Amazon should sell groceries from neighborhood markets. What are the pros and cons of this idea?

CANDIDATE: I want to make sure I understand the concept fully. A customer can go to the Amazon website, purchase groceries and collect their purchase from their local store?

INTERVIEWER: That's correct. Their purchases will be picked for them and be waiting for them within 30 minutes.

CANDIDATE: Give me a moment to collect my thoughts.

INTERVIEWER: Sure.

Candidate pauses for 20 seconds

CANDIDATE: And I envision the customer benefit including:

- **Amazon shopping experience**: product details, inventory availability, reviews, and forums.
- **Lists**: ability to save most commonly purchased items.
- **Fulfillment speed**: ability to get products within a 1 hr. time window. No need to wait for the Amazon Fresh truck.

INTERVIEWER: Correct, and what would be the benefit to Amazon?

CANDIDATE: Amazon would get the following benefits:

- **Improved customer experience**: getting products a lot faster than their typical 2-5 day ship times.
- **Save on shipping fees**: customers picking up their own products.
- **Make money**: Amazon getting a cut of the transaction since it is driving more business to local stores.

148

INTERVIEWER: Okay, there's a lot of upside in this plan, both for customers, Amazon and local stores. What do you anticipate the top three issues to be?

CANDIDATE: Here's what I think are the top issues:

1. **Signing up local stores.** Amazon doesn't have relationships with local stores today. Amazon will have to spend considerable effort to sign up stores. It could be a while before Amazon gets a significant local store network.
2. **Local store integration.** Many of the local stores may have trouble integrating with Amazon's ordering systems. Many local stores may not have technical know-how or time for integration.
3. **Quality risk.** The local store's products may not be the same quality that customers expect from Amazon.
4. **Inventory data.** For this idea to succeed, Amazon needs to report accurate inventory data from local stores. It would be very frustrating for customers if a product is reported as available, but is not.
5. **Inventory availability.** Amazon can aggregate so much demand. Local stores may not have the inventory to fulfill.
6. **Competitive risk.** Customer can choose to bypass Amazon and buy directly from the local merchant in the future.

INTERVIEWER: You're an overachiever, huh? I like that. So out of your list of 6 items, what do you think is the biggest risk?

CANDIDATE: All of the items sound challenging. However, I think inventory availability is the biggest risk. It's hard to forecast demand for a product. I don't think local stores can scale inventory as quick as we'd like, especially with the customer traffic that Amazon can bring to customers.

Comments: Candidate does a good job summarizing the customer and business benefit of the new proposal. The candidate is great with summarizing the top issues. However, when asked to pick the most pressing issue, his pick of "inventory availability" seems arbitrary and ultimately unconvincing.

Chapter 13 Strategizing: CEO-level Issues

How to Approach CEO-level Strategy Questions

Strategy questions on CEO-level issues usually relate to:

- Competitive issues
- Acquisition opportunities
- Complementary products
- Corporate values

It's not necessary to memorize separate frameworks for each CEO-level issue. Use the shorthand that most executives use. Start by thinking how these companies make money and the critical drivers to the business. Then, consider how the competition, the new acquisition, or complementary product can affect those particular business drivers.

Practice Questions

1. You're Larry Page. The head of corporate development tells you that Quora is in play, and both Microsoft and Facebook are bidding for it. Should Google participate in the discussions? Why?

2. You are the CEO of the Yellow Cab taxi service. How do you respond to Uber?

3. If you were Google's CEO, would you be concerned about Microsoft?

4. How does Google make money, and what are the biggest threats?

5. How does LinkedIn make money, and what are the biggest threats?

6. Google launched a new program: Google Trusted Stores. Why is Google Trusted Stores strategically important for the company?

7. Should Amazon launch a smartphone?

8. Choose a company that you believe provides a world-class customer experience. What do they do well?

Answers

You're Larry Page. The head of corporate development tells you that Quora is in play, and both Microsoft and Facebook are bidding for it. Should Google participate in the discussions? Why?

CANDIDATE: Yes. There are three reasons why Google should participate in the acquisition discussions.

1. **Quora's content is valuable.** When doing longtail informational searches, Quora often offers the best result, especially around business, psychology and entrepreneurship.

2. **Hold-up threat.** If Quora's valuable content ends up in the hands of competitors, such as Microsoft or Facebook, both companies can prevent Google from indexing Quora's content and making it available in Google's search results.

3. **Threat to Google's search brand.** Google wants to maintain a reputation as the first place to find anything on the web. Increasingly, Quora is building a reputation for the first place to find business, entrepreneurship and psychology advice. If this reputation solidifies, Google will lose its "first-stop" status and be relegated to a subset of all information searches.

Comments: Candidate does a good job articulating the benefits of a Quora acquisition. He keenly identifies the risk of not having Quora content available. But there are some areas of improvement. Quora is not an acceptable acquisition at any price. The candidate should at least acknowledge pricing as a key issue, if not propose a back of the envelope calculation on what is a reasonable acquisition price. Also, the candidate neglects to mention the cons of doing the deal. By presenting an imbalanced view, it invites the interviewer to come up with challenger statements on her own, which makes the interviewer feel that the candidate's argument is less compelling.

You are the CEO of the Yellow Cab taxi service. How do you respond to Uber?

CANDIDATE: I apologize, but I'm never used the Uber service. Can you tell me more about it?

INTERVIEWER: Uber allows users to request, ride, and pay for black car, like a taxi, service using a mobile phone.

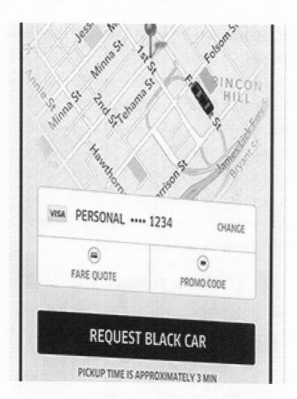

The first value proposition is convenience. You can request a car with a single button tap. No more calling the dispatcher and waiting in line.

The second value proposition is reliability. You know that your driver is coming and how far they are from you. No more guessing if the driver is going to show up in 5 minutes, 30 minutes or not at all.

The third value proposition is clear pricing. With a well-defined range, there's no more guessing whether your cab ride is going to cost $15 or $85.

CANDIDATE: Is Uber cheaper than a Yellow Taxi?

INTERVIEWER: Sometimes it is, and sometimes it isn't. Low price is not a value proposition that Uber advertises.

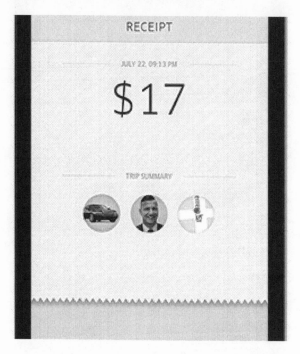

The fourth value proposition is cashless transactions. No more "Can you drop me off at the ATM?" to get cash or worry about handing credit card details to the driver.

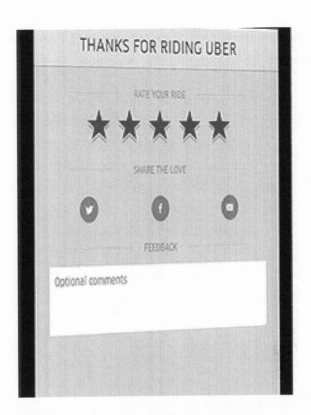

The fifth value proposition is that feedback matters.

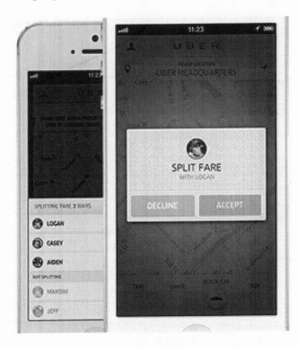

The last value proposition is that it's very easy to split the fare with other Uber users.

CANDIDATE: Thanks for walking me through the product. If I were to compare my Yellow Cab experiences with Uber, Uber's most compelling value proposition is reliability. I can't tell you how many times I've called Yellow Cab and it's either late or never shows up. If I'm trying to catch a flight, not having my ride show up on time or at all, is far from acceptable. And when I call the dispatcher, they're usually unmotivated, low paid employees. They either make up an estimated time to arrival. They waste valuable time trying to chase down the driver, get the estimated time to arrival, and communicate it back to the customer – while dealing with 1000 other things at the office.

I feel Uber's reliability and driver monitoring is the main reason why the service is successful. Also there's no need to recite and confirm starting and ending destinations, which can commonly get garbled over a bad phone connection.

As the Yellow Cab CEO, I would work quickly to solve this reliability and monitoring problem.

INTERVIEWER: Are you sure this is how the Yellow Cab CEO would want to respond? Wouldn't they much rather sue Uber on the grounds that Uber drivers aren't properly licensed?

CANDIDATE: As CEO, I would pursue all tools to preserve corporate profits. However, I would have to have a plan B in case the judicial system deems that they are legitimate competitors.

INTERVIEWER: Okay, continue.

CANDIDATE: Just to recap, Uber exploited the smartphone & Google Maps revolution by bypassing the taxi dispatcher. By having customers receive communications directly from drivers, Uber increased reliability of their car services.

To respond, we need to improve our reliability by giving real time data on where our drivers are and how soon they will get to the user's location.

I have a couple of ideas in mind:

1. **Partner with Uber**. Allow Yellow Cab customers to hail Yellow Cab taxis on Uber's app. Provide all the benefits of Uber, including real-time monitoring, cashless transactions, etc. For Uber, partnering expands their fleet and minimizes the regulatory scrutiny around the service. The downside is that Uber owns the customer relationship. Uber will also build their brand as the destination for hailing a car. Yellow Cab risks being a commodity supplier that can be replaced any other taxi or car service.

2. **Develop a Yellow Cab app**. The app would offer all the benefits of the Uber app. The good news: Yellow Cab's brand has high recognition. Users would quickly install the app. Early tech adopters would be familiar with the core functionality because they've used or heard of Uber. However, to my knowledge, Yellow Cab doesn't have tech competency, so they would either have to outsource the tech development or build a tech team. This is riskier than it seems.

3. **Develop a SMS service where customers can get Yellow Cabs**. This option provides the taxi monitoring benefit of the app, while extending the value beyond smartphone owners. Smartphone penetration is about 61 percent. However, SMS penetration is even higher at 87 percent. Of course, it poses similar technical risks, to Yellow Cab, as developing an app.

Out of these ideas, which one would you pursue?

Given Yellow Cab's strong brand name, I don't think partnering is necessary in the long-term. They could partner with Uber in the short-term to get the service going and then in the long-term build their own Uber-like platform in-house. This is similar to the late 90s where Target and Toys R Us utilized Amazon's eCommerce platform temporarily before in-housing that capability. That choice didn't weaken Target or Toys R Us eCommerce prospects in the long-term.

And assuming current licensing laws hold, Yellow Cab shouldn't be concerned about being commoditized. Taxi licensing laws prevent an influx of competition (when enforced, of course). Customers will use whatever app that will provide access to reliable taxis.

Comments: Candidate does a good job understanding two things:

1. **The primary Uber value proposition is about reliability, despite the other benefits.**
2. **Uber's technology disruption centered on one of the weakest links in the taxicab process, the dispatcher.**

Candidate's ideas for improving reliability and cutting out the dispatcher are well reasoned.

If you were Google's CEO, would you be concerned about Microsoft?

CANDIDATE: Aside from competitive strengths and resources, Microsoft is a threat because it controls two of Google's distribution on-ramps: Internet Explorer and Windows. Internet Explorer is one of the biggest on-ramps to the web, where Google makes money from advertising. Microsoft also controls Windows, which is one of the biggest operating system on-ramps to a browser.

Google must protect itself from being locked out of distribution onramps. A number of things it should and has done:

- Protect default search settings on any browser platform
- Create its own browser alternative
- Create its own operating system on PCs, smartphones and other devices that display Google advertising

Microsoft also competes directly with several Google businesses including search, search and display advertising, and office productivity software and servers. In most of these businesses Microsoft is either first or second with lots of employees and significant financial resources behind each one.

Lastly, Microsoft has an impressive partner and sales ecosystem. Their sales force has relationships with a broad spectrum of IT decision makers. And their partner ecosystem ranges from OEMs, retailers, and IT consulting firms.

Comments: Porter's five forces is a convenient checklist when thinking about competitive threats. For example, access to distribution channels, size of competition, and Microsoft's differentiation, in terms of partner and sales ecosystem, are inferred in the candidate's response.

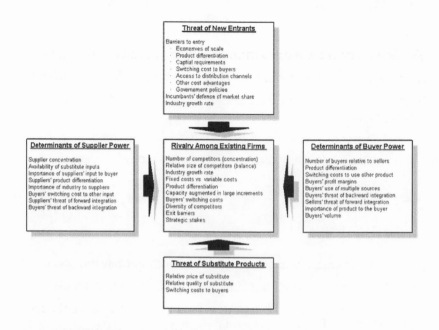

How does Google make money, and what are the biggest threats?

CANDIDATE: Can I have a moment to think about it?

INTERVIEWER: Sure.

Candidate takes 30 seconds.

CANDIDATE: I did some research on Google's business model, and they make about $18 billion per year. Most of that comes from online advertising. Only $1 billion comes from sales of other products such as Google Apps.

When I think about Google's biggest challenges, the first three that come to mind are mobile ads, social networks, and mobile phones.

	Demand Side Issues	Supply Side Issues
Mobile Ads	Low monetization	Limited inventory
Social Networks	Spare target data	Do not own the leading social network
Mobile Phones	Brand	Vertical integration

162

The first threat is mobile advertising. Google's business is changing from a PC to a mobile centric world. Latest industry data from Marin Software shows that mobile impressions grew from 12.5% in 2012 to 24.7% in 2013.

However, the cost per click for a mobile ad is about 15% lower than desktop ads. On the demand side, there are many reasons why mobile advertisements don't sell as well: low commercial intent, small display, and poor targeting options.

On the supply side, the migration from PC to mobile has impact as well. On the PC, users see ads primarily on websites. On a mobile device, users see ads on both websites and apps. Google does not have advertising relationships with the thousands of new app developers, creating opportunities for competitors to create mobile ad networks.

As a result, Google's share of the mobile ad impressions is not as dominant as it is on the PC. Google can't offer the one-stop shop buy-all-your-ads-here value proposition that Google offered in the PC world.

The second threat is social networks. Google+ is the 2nd largest social network after Facebook. However, Google+ does not have as much profile or behavioral data as Facebook. These data gaps could lead to ineffective ads and lower monetization potential.

The other problem is that Google does not own ad inventory on the world's dominant social network. While Google's advertisers can participate on the Facebook Ad Exchange, Google are subject to Facebook's rules, leading to supply risk.

The third threat is mobile phones. Android does have 75% worldwide market share. However, among consumers, Android is perceived as the cheap brand while Apple is perceived as the premium brand. This limits the available profits in the Android ecosystem. In other words, margins are slim.

On the product side, Android has two main problems. Firstly, aside from the Motorola division, Google does build Android phones from start-to-finish. That is, Android software is produced by Google, but the hardware is developed by third party partners such as Samsung and HTC. This additional cross-company coordination leads to products that aren't as thoughtfully designed as products offered from a single company like Apple.

Secondly, each Android manufacturer has the power to determine how to customize the Android devices for their own handsets. This leads to product fragmentation, which could damage the customer experience and Android's brand reputation.

Comments: Candidate offered a very thoughtful discussion around Google's key challenges. The supply and demand side framework was simply effective. It forced the candidate to think through various dimensions of each issue, creating a complete and satisfying response.

How does LinkedIn make money, and what are the biggest threats?

CANDIDATE: I did some research on this last night. Here's the breakdown if I remember correctly:

LinkedIn Revenue Streams

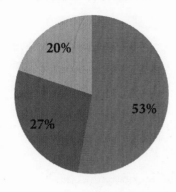

INTERVIEWER: What are the different divisions?

CANDIDATE: Talent Solutions help organizations find and acquire talent. For example, LinkedIn Recruiter allows recruiters to search, view, and contact every profile that's usually restricted in the free offering. And Talent Solutions offer project management functionality to add notes and reminders to key candidates for follow-up.

Marketing Solutions includes ads, sponsorships, custom groups and customization of LinkedIn's InMails. Ads can be targeted based on user's profile information.

Lastly, Premium Subscriptions offer features to help individuals and businesses to manage their professional identity, grow their business, and connect with talent. This includes features to see profile information for 3rd degree contacts, send InMails to people they're not connected with, and see stats on who is viewing their profile.

INTERVIEWER: Ok, so what are the biggest threats to LinkedIn?

CANDIDATE: I'll classify the competitive threats by divisions:

1. For the Premium Subscriptions team, the threats are niche professional networks. For example, GitHub and Dribbble are thriving social networks for developers and designers respectively. Each audience has specific needs, and both GItHub and Dribbble have created functionality to better meet those needs.
2. For Marketing Solutions, the threat is traditional advertisers like Google and Facebook. With behavioral targeting, advertisers can likely reach similar audiences that LinkedIn can.
3. For Hiring Solutions, I imagine Web 1.0 methods of identifying candidates, such as hiring portals from Monster.com and HotJobs, would be the prime competitors.

INTERVIEWER: How should LinkedIn respond niche professional networks like GitHub?

CANDIDATE: Give me a moment to collect my thoughts.

Takes a 30 second pause.

CANDIDATE: I'm not a GitHub user, but if I were to imagine the three main needs of the GitHub audience, here's what I would say:

1. **Collaboration**. It allows teams to easily manage code within organizations. Source control, revision history, and access control lists are some key features that enable collaboration among developers.
2. **Community**. Each developer gets a profile page where they can connect with other developers and projects. It's a great way to identify talented developers and possibly talent.
3. **Feedback**. Users can identify which repositories they're working on or following. With open repositories, other users can comment on their work and possibly improve their code.

LinkedIn's best response is to offer features that address these needs that aren't currently being addressed by LinkedIn today. For instance:

- **Project repository**. Provide free storage to post their work on LinkedIn. Allow users to link to showcase the work from LinkedIn.
- **Community**. Allow users to get feedback on their work. Have permissive creative commons licensing options where users can expand on a user's work and make it etter.
- **Collaboration**. Give users an option to collaborate. For example, solicit or hire LinkedIn experts to help improve what they're doing.

For each one of these product improvements, the PM team can choose to build, buy, or partner. For example, they could partner with GitHub to easily share their GitHub repositories on LinkedIn.

Comments: The candidate did his homework and researched LinkedIn's revenue streams. Most candidates would have kept it short and vague such as "advertising and premium subscriptions." This candidate took a competitor-centric approach to identifying threats. This is different from a customer or market trends we had seen earlier. We see that it works quite well. Candidate distilled the key shortcomings of LinkedIn vs. these niche professional networks for niche audiences. He gives the interviewer confidence that he will have a reasonable plan to approach the problem.

Google launched a new program: Google Trusted Stores. Why is Google Trusted Stores strategically important for the company?

CANDIDATE: Before I jump in, do you mind if I ask some questions about Google Trusted Stores? I'm not familiar with this program.

INTERVIEWER: Sure.

CANDIDATE: What is Google Trusted Stores?

INTERVIEWER: Google Trusted Stores is an ecommerce certification program. It identifies which merchants offer a good shopping experience.

For example, when a Google search user sees an ad, there's an icon that indicates that it is a Google Trusted Store.

The user can hover over the name and get more information about the program:

As you can see, Google gives this certification to shippers with reliable shipping and excellent service. Google will also offer to be a third-party mediator and offer up to $1,000 protection for your purchase.

CANDIDATE: Okay, give me a moment to collect my thoughts on the topic.

Candidate writes the following:

- *User*
- *Advertiser*
- *Competition*
- *Google*

CANDIDATE: Okay, you'd like me to discuss the strategic value of the Google Trusted Stores concept. Here's how I would approach it. I'd first explore how this program impacts the Google search user. Then I'd evaluate how this helps our customer, the advertiser. Lastly, I'd want to see how this protects Google from the competition and lastly, how this helps Google's core business. Is there anything else that you'd like me to cover?

INTERVIEWER: Are you planning to come up with a dollar value for the program?

CANDIDATE: I wasn't planning to, but I can if you'd like.

INTERVIEWER: That's not necessary. A qualitative discussion is fine.

CANDIDATE: Okay, let's start with the user. For the user, the Google Trusted Store badge gives me buying confidence, especially a retailer that doesn't have a big brand name. It's similar to a Better Business Bureau (BBB) seal. If I do a transaction, I will likely get the product I was promised, in a timely manner, without excessive hassle.

Given the assurance, I'm more likely to return to Google again to shop. That is, click on ads and complete purchases (i.e. conversions).

Candidate summaries on the whiteboard:

- *More visits to Google search*
- *More clicks on ads*
- *More conversions*

CANDIDATE: For the advertiser, there are several benefits.

Candidate writes on the whiteboard:

- *More clicks*
- *More conversions*

CANDIDATE: The Google Trusted Store badge stands out from other ads. For users who are unfamiliar with the badge, they'll likely click on it out of curiosity. For users who are familiar with the badge, they'll also likely click on it, but because they know it's a symbol of quality.

This will give that advertiser a higher share of clicks for that search query. That's incredibly valuable because it solves a Google advertiser's number one problem: not enough clicks! Anything they can do to get more sales, as long as it's ROI positive, they will do it.

Conversions are also likely to go up because the user has fewer qualms about purchasing from a smaller brand merchant. That's great news for the advertiser. Not only do they like more sales, but also they like that every advertising dollar is likely to drive more sales. In other words, advertising ROI goes up.

This improves Google's eCommerce shopping experience, when compared to a shopping experience on Amazon or eBay. I'll tell you how.

Candidate writes on the whiteboard:

- *Trust*
- *Brand*
- *Advertiser dollars*

The first issue is trust. Users can be wary of clicking ads or buying from Google merchants because they've never heard of them or the merchant's storefront is unprofessional.

The second issue is brand. Google could be perceived as a site where consumers research purchases, but when it comes to purchase, they should go to somewhere where they can shop with confidence, whether it's a branded big box retailer like Target or Best Buy or an online shopping mall like Amazon marketplace.

If the reputation sticks, then consumers are less likely to click on Google's ads and complete transactions, which hurt Google's cost per click business model.

The third issue is advertiser dollars. Advertisers have many options to drive traffic to their website. For example, they can create stores at

Amazon marketplace, eBay stores, or Etsy. Or they can advertise at competitive search engines, such as Bing or Yahoo.

If Google's users don't click on ads or do without purchasing anything, then advertisers will not be satisfied with their ROI. If their advertising dollars aren't efficient, they'll look for other alternatives.

The last thing I wanted to evaluate: how does Google Trusted Stores benefit Google's long-term strategy? For Google to report shipping satisfaction on its website, the merchant shares shipment and cancellation information with Google.

This information tells Google whether a conversion occurred, helping Google understand the effectiveness of their advertising offerings. This data can be used to develop new Google products, such as advertising based on a pay-per-sale business model or tweak Google's algorithms on which retargeted products to show to a Google user, based on the propensity to convert, based on the Trusted Store feed.

Comments: Candidate wasn't familiar with the product, but did an excellent job clarifying what it was before laying out a clear, easy-to-follow framework to assess the program's value to Google. The response's depth shows how well the candidate understands Google's business and the program's strategic value.

Should Amazon launch a smartphone?

CANDIDATE: I'd like to answer this question by first reviewing our objective, whether it's revenue, customer satisfaction or loyalty. Then, I'll talk about the customer pain points, see if this is in-line with Amazon's strengths, and then review the market trends.

Today's mobile phone customer has a two-year contract subsidy, and it includes only so many minutes. There's a slight movement toward prepaid, but not much.

Phone selection is fairly limited. There's Apple, Google and Nokia, which will soon be Microsoft.

Amazon's strengths include a large customer base. Last time I heard they've got 30 million customers. They've got a marketplace full of books, music, and movies that can be digitally loaded onto the device. Also, they have a powerful network of affiliates. But Amazon does have several weaknesses when it comes to selling a phone. First, Amazon has no brick and mortar locations, so customers can't test their smartphone. Second, Amazon doesn't have any experience building phones. Third, they've got a good eCommerce brand, but it's not clear that Amazon's brand can extend into smartphones too.

I feel Amazon can also subsidize the cost of the device by giving offers or showing ads. And if Amazon's foray into tablets is any indication, the Amazon smartphone is likely to have a decent form factor.

The key market trend is that more people are buying products using their smartphone.

My recommendation is that Amazon should pursue this opportunity. Offer the phones on contract to lower the price of the hardware, and optimize the phone for easy purchase of digital goods via Amazon's marketplace.

Comments: The answer sounds okay, but it's very flawed. The candidate completely missed the strategic importance of launching a smartphone, which is to protect Amazon's physical media revenue (books, music, movies).

Books, music and movies are being sold digitally and consumers are buying them through its competitors: Apple's iTunes and Google Play.

Candidate attempts to use a framework, but it's purely mechanical.

Choose a company that you believe provides a world-class customer experience. What do they do well?

CANDIDATE: Home Depot has a world-class customer experience. When I think why, it comes down to three criteria:

- How knowledgeable is the staff?
- Does the staff go the extra mile to help me out?
- Can I find the product I need?

I'll go into more detail. Let's say I have a home improvement problem, but I don't know how to solve it. Without knowing what to solve, I don't know what to buy at Home Depot. Because their staff is very knowledgeable, often staffed with former contractors, they both point you to the product you need and give you tips. For customers who are looking for solutions, it's a blessing that the staff doesn't just care about selling products, but solving problems.

The staff typically goes an extra mile to help you out. The other day, I needed to buy a hex wrench to loosen up my sink disposal. The Home Depot clerk and I weren't too sure of which one I should buy. Rather than have me buy a couple wrenches and return the ones that didn't work, he said, "Let's take all these to the sink disposal section and make sure we find a good fit before you checkout." It required him to open up some packaging to do so. I really appreciated his extra effort.

Lastly, I can always find the home improvement product that I need at Home Depot. I'm always rest assured that my time driving to Home Depot is time well spent.

INTERVIEWER: What's an example of a company that has a poor customer experience?

CANDIDATE: Give me a moment to think about it.

Candidate takes 10 seconds.

CANDIDATE: I didn't have to look too far. Lowe's provides a poor customer experience. And here's why:

Understaffed. Home improvement purchases are complicated. Customers need help — whether it's to identify the right product or picking the right product from the top shelf. Lowe's stores are consistently understaffed that customers, on average, spend 3 to 5 minutes searching for an associate to assist. Compared to Home Depot, where associates are plentiful and can be often found in less than 30 seconds, providing customers with more pleasing experiences.

Lowe's sales associates are poorly trained. Many of them seem to be new and don't understand Lowe's processes. I've had two occasions where they did a poor job describing how sales discounts are being applied.

Limited product selection. I've had a hard time finding the right products in the store; they don't seem to have Home Depot's extensive product selection.

To improve the situation, I would recommend the following be addressed:

Improve sales associate knowledge. Either hiring more skilled clerks or better training programs can accomplish this. A recent MSN Money poll mentioned that knowledgeable staff is what customers say matters most.

Hire more associates. Customers don't like to waste time. Make it easy for customers to get questions answered. An alternative to hiring associates could include self-service information kiosks, more product pamphlets, better signage and a system to locate and page the nearest sales associate.

Increase product selection. Product selection is key. It can be improved by either carrying more goods in-store, supplement in-store goods with goods that can be purchased online or possibly partner with complementary partners that would give Lowe's a more complete solution set for customers.

Comments: Aside from the detail, what makes this response believable is that this is the candidate's own personal experiences. He answers the question with conviction. He presents her criteria for what makes a good response at the beginning. Lastly, he makes some good recommendations on how Lowe's can improve their customer service.

Chapter 14 Creating Vision

Several top tech companies, including Google and Facebook, care about a candidate's ability to have a compelling product vision. It's important for three reasons:

Thinking big. Many product management candidates default to "me too" innovation. That is, a social network should be designed like Facebook, and a mobile phone should look like an Apple iPhone.

However, given the barriers to entry, it is unlikely users will switch to a competitive product that's simply a clone of the market leader. Users will only switch if a product is better. And that type of improvement comes only when the product leaders think big.

Influence and morale. Product managers lead teams. Product managers are more likely to get things done through a team if he or she can communicate a product goal that's innovative.

Credibility. A good vision is one that's aggressively big. However, at the same time, it's seemingly doable. In May 1961, President John F. Kennedy proclaimed:

"First, I believe that this nation should commit itself to achieving the goal, before this decade is out, of landing a man on the moon and returning him safely to the Earth."

It was a grand vision. No man or animal had been to the moon and back. But it was seemingly doable. The previous month, John Glenn, had been the first American to venture to and from space. So this idea of going to the moon — seemed both attainable and worth fighting for, despite an aggressive timeline.

How to Approach Vision Questions

1. **Solve a problem**. The vision must solve a real problem. Pursuits that are cool aren't worthwhile. This problem also needs to be big. It has to solve a problem for billions of people or dollars.

2. **Be unique and memorable**. Most candidates answer vision questions with the first idea in their heads. More often than not, their answer is "tighter integration between two products." Not only is it not compelling, but it's not unique or memorable. Good visions move us. We obsess over them. We can't wait to share those bold visions with our friends and colleagues.

3. **Describe how it will be solved**. There are two parts to a good vision response, and it includes both the vision and how it will be accomplished. Each part should have equal air time. A response with the first part, but without the second will not stick. The vision will be derided as a pipe dream. The burden is on you. Convince us that it's doable and go into specifics.

Practice Question

1. Choose one of these verticals. Where do you think it'll be in ten years?

Answer

Choose one of these verticals. Where do you think it'll be in ten years?

Interviewer writes on the board:

- *3D Printing*
- *Education*
- *Energy*
- *Mobile*

- *Security*

INTERVIEWER: Choose one of these five verticals. Where do you think it'll be in ten years?

CANDIDATE: Hmm, I'll choose education. I love my kids, and I think about how hard it is for them to learn. The oldest is trying to memorize a Chinese poem. Yesterday, she cried and cried because she couldn't do it. She wanted to give up.

I gave her a tip: memorize the poem in chunks. It worked. It was easier to memorize bite-sized pieces of information and she memorized the entire poem within one hour.

So, to answer your question, I think in the next ten years there's a huge opportunity to create the AllRecipes.com of learning; that is, every single lesson plan from every single teacher around the world can be indexed on a single website.

We would develop a PageRank-like formula to determine the most effective way to teach a concept. It would accelerate the learning process exponentially. Who knows? Rather than spend 13 years to get through K-12 education, what if we could teach everyone the same material in just 5 years?

INTERVIEWER: K-12 in just 5 years? Impossible.

CANDIDATE: It's a moonshot. I'll tell you why I'm confident it might work. There are 5,000 characters in the Chinese language, but here's the interesting thing: 300 Chinese characters are used in 65 percent of all discussions. Research has found that it's easier to master Chinese if one focuses on knowing just those 300 characters really well and inferring the rest through context.

In one week, one can comprehend 85 percent of 300 Chinese characters. Alternatively, it'll take three years to learn all 5,000 characters, increasing comprehension by only 5 percent.

The key is in knowing which 300 characters to learn. That's what this website will help us determine, effective ways to teach.

INTERVIEWER: Okay, good learning methods make a difference; but the challenge is getting all the lesson plans out of teachers' brains and into an indexed system. How are you going to do that?

CANDIDATE: The biggest barrier is documenting lesson plans and teaching methods. Jack Welch can be a great leader, but he can't teach leadership, despite all the books he's written. You see that time and time again: Many authors can't teach success. On the opposite end of the spectrum, third-party sources try to document and teach greatness, and they fall short. For example, many authors have tried to capture Warren Buffett's greatness, but fall short.

INTERVIEWER: Okay, so what's your magic solution?

CANDIDATE: There's a new technology that has a lot of promise: the Brain Cap. A University of Washington researcher invented it. It is a computer that can detect brain waves for thoughts and actions. Once the brain waves are recorded, they can be saved or transmitted to another person.

The Brain Cap is still in the early stages of development, but there's potential. If we could constantly monitor and document teachers' thoughts and techniques, we could create the world's most effective database of lesson plans, cut down on learning time, and improve efficacy. This could be the biggest breakthrough for knowledge dissemination and learning since the Internet.

Comments: Well done. The candidate led with a personal hook into an industry he's passionate about. Indexing all the lesson plans on the planet is a real problem and an audacious goal. The candidate clearly articulates the technology gap that enables the vision and introduces an early-stage invention that's a plausible and impactful solution.

What do you think LinkedIn can do on the iPhone that is truly groundbreaking?

CANDIDATE: When I think about LinkedIn, there's one thing I can do on my computer but I can't do on my iPhone: view LinkedIn profiles in my mail client.

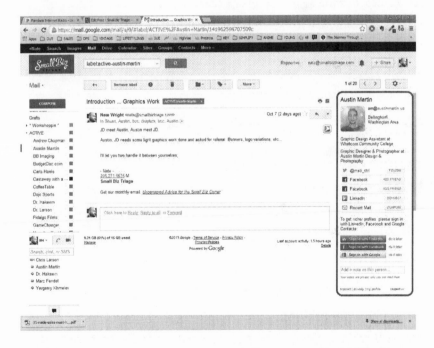

Using the Rapportive plug-in, my Gmail client can pull in LinkedIn information to the right of my email. It provides valuable context on whom I am emailing, what they do, and links to their social profiles.

From: iCloud ›   Hide

To:

Your complimentary iCloud storage upgrade has been extended at no charge

October 5, 2012, 6:13 PM

Dear Jason Grigsby,

When you moved your MobileMe account to iCloud, we provided you with a complimentary storage upgrade beyond the standard 5GB that comes with an iCloud account to help you with the transition. Originally, this storage upgrade was set to expire on September 30, 2012.

By comparison, the iPhone mail client doesn't have as much contextual information. There's a lot of potential to have LinkedIn information within a mobile email app.

There are three different ways to solve this. First, we can maintain the status quo and have users toggle between their current smartphone mail client and the LinkedIn app or website if they're looking for more information. While the solution is available today, the downside is that this is cumbersome for the user to toggle between multiple apps on their phone.

Second, we can create a new iPhone mail application which augments emails with LinkedIn information. The good news: it circumvents restrictions one would encounter within an iPhone mail client. Apple is notorious for having a closed ecosystem and blocking other apps from interfering from the core experience. Apple meticulously avoids the fragmentation that plagues operating systems such as Android, where the operating system varies based on the manufacturer and the model. The bad news is that many iPhone users are accustomed to using the iPhone mail app already and are unlikely to switch.

The third option is to have LinkedIn information in the existing the iPhone mail app. It's least disruptive of all the solutions; it doesn't require users to learn a new app. However, it could present some technical challenges.

INTERVIEWER: The 3rd option is impossible. Apple does not have an API for adding information into the built-in iPhone mail app. I understand you want to provide something that's new and useful, but I don't see how something like this could happen.

CANDIDATE: It does seem unlikely, but I believe we can do it without having API access to Apple's mail client. I've given it some thought on how I would implement this.

First, I'd want a dynamic UI. When minimized, I could see at a glance the person's photo, title, and past roles. However, I can tap to expand and see more information including LinkedIn connections, summary, and experience.

Second, I'd want dynamic content. Within the UI, I should have the options to connect with a LinkedIn contact. That's the easy part. Today, we could do that by simply going to Safari. But here's where it gets interesting: the next time I open the same email, I shouldn't have an option to connect to the same person again, since I did it already. Instead, the mail should reflect different relationship statuses including: connect, invited, and already connected.

Lastly, I need the Apple client to add all this additional information without using an API.

INTERVIEWER: Ok, so where is this going?

CANDIDATE: Let me explain the technical solution that makes this happen. For the third item, I found that while we could not add to the mail client, we could modify the messages themselves. We can store the modified version of the message on a proxy server.

Only the user's iPhone mail client would connect to the proxy server and serve up the LinkedIn-enhanced version of the message. If the user is viewing the same message on Gmail on their laptop, they would get the original, unenhanced version on the regular Gmail server.

One of the benefits of the proxy server approach: we know exactly what device is downloading message, so we can adapt the layout to the right screen size without worrying about compatibility with other devices.

For the first problem, you're probably thinking that we can't render JavaScript inside the iPhone mail client. And you're right. However, the iPhone mail client does render CSS. And CSS does have a :hover state. On a mobile Safari browser rendering engine, which the iPhone mail client uses, has a unique interpretation of the :hover state. There's no hovering on a mobile device. So tapping once, is equivalent to hovering over a link. And tapping twice is equivalent to selecting a link. By using this insight, we've enabled an interactive UI in the iPhone mail client. You can tap once to expand a LinkedIn profile. And tap twice to minimize it.

For the second problem, we need the message to check your relationship with the connection every time the email is opened. We can easily have the message check the server by having the status icon be represented as an <iframe>. Every time the mail is opened, the <iframe> would load the newest state. And if the device is offline, the

<iframe> part of the message would simply default to the last known state.

INTERVIEWER: That's a pretty audacious vision. I can see how you could fulfill it, especially with those Apple hacks. Good job.

Comments: The candidate presents an useful, but seemingly unattainable product vision. The candidate deftly convinces that his vision is doable by technically explaining how his vision could be achieved. This probably goes into more technical detail than your typical interview response, but was necessary to convince a skeptical interviewer.

Adapted from the article: http://linkd.in/1cKcGzB

Chapter 15 Passing the Stress Test

Hiring managers want to gauge how you handle stressful situations. Some interviewers would ask behavioral questions such as,

- Tell me a time when you were overwhelmed at work. How did you cope?
- Tell me a time when you had a difficult deadline. How did you react?

However, some interviewers are concerned that a candidate's responses could be canned. Instead, they prefer a stress simulation at the interview. That is, ask an interview question that puts the candidate in an uncomfortable situation and see how they respond. This may involve using questions that have no right answer, with the interviewer playing the obnoxious devil's advocate to see whether you waffle or become defensive. Here are examples of how an interviewer might stress you during the interview:

Hypothetical Question	"An executive lied to cover up a mistake. Would you report him or her?"
Reaction to An Interview Response	"That's your best management story? It doesn't sound like you have a lot of experience. I was expecting a story where you fired someone."

How to Approach the Stress Test

Understand why the interviewer would ask these questions.

More often than not, this is about cultural fit. That is, do you espouse and demonstrate the employer's corporate values? Some corporations look for candidates who aren't afraid of speaking up, even when it means contradicting a respected executive. Other employers want candidates who can adopt mindsets that aren't their own but might originate from someone else in the company.

To summarize, prepare by understanding the corporate values. It'll give you clues on what they expect in a good response.

Manage the stress.

The interview is stressful enough as it is. Having a skeptical and possibly obnoxious interviewer makes it more difficult.

To manage the stress, use a technique called exposure therapy. That is, find a friend before the interview. Have that friend be the tough interviewer. After a couple of exposures, your heart will be less likely to race when someone gives you a tough time. You'll realize what everyone else realizes during the stress interview: you'll survive.

Separate the question from the emotion.

After the initial emotional flood triggers you, approach the question in an objective, intellectually curious way. If you think the question is meant to torture, let those thoughts go.

All of these questions are valid. For example, it's someone's job to determine whether or not to be a whistleblower on a cheating executive. Or, despite the blunt delivery, it's also fair for the interviewer to tell you that they've heard better answers to the same question.

Release the emotion. Focus back on what the interviewer is saying, openly approach the question, think through your response and construct a thoughtful, objective answer.

Practice Question

1. Look at this diagram. Where would you place yourself, and why?

Answer

Look at this diagram. Where would you place yourself, and why?

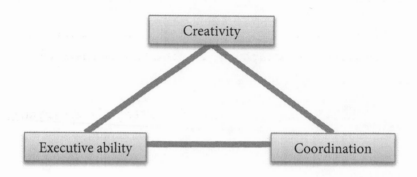

Candidate pauses briefly and flashes a concerned "uh oh" look.

CANDIDATE: I would place myself here.

Candidate adds a dot near the middle of the graph:

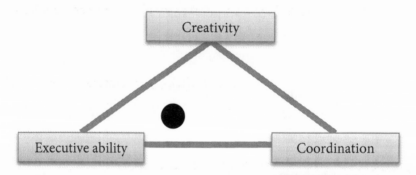

CANDIDATE: I put myself there is for the following reasons:

	Example
Executive ability	As an Apple product manager, I could really execute. I got a lot of stuff done in a short period of time.
Coordination	When I worked at HP, I was a great coordinator. I had great relationships.

Creativity	I am creative at work and at home. I compete in hackathons and have come up with lots of cool apps.

INTERVIEWER: That doesn't make any sense. Executive ability isn't about execution.

CANDIDATE: Oh.

INTERVIEWER: Also, the dot is far away from coordination and creativity. So are you saying that you're not creative and have bad coordination?

CANDIDATE: I'm not saying that. No one can be perfect at everything.

INTERVIEWER: You just agreed with my point. And your tone of voice is very defensive.

CANDIDATE: You're right. I got a bit emotional about it. I apologize. Do you mind if I reset & start over?

INTERVIEW: Uh, okay.

CANDIDATE: All right, so I understand that you want to see where I rank along these labels. Do you mind if I ask a few clarifying questions?

INTERVIEWER: Sure.

CANDIDATE: I understand creativity, but I don't understand the other two labels. Can you explain what you mean by coordination and executive ability?

INTERVIEWER: Executive ability refers to your ability to make difficult decisions and sway others to your vision or point of view. Coordination is a measure of your ability to get things done, which includes your perseverance.

CANIDDATE: You only want me to assess these three characteristics and not other strengths and weaknesses of mine?

INTERVIEWER: Correct.

CANDIDATE: Here's my first observation about this exercise: I don't think there are necessarily tradeoffs between any of these three labels. That is, someone can be strong in creativity, executive ability and coordination, but this diagram doesn't allow for this possibility.

INTERVIEWER: That's an interesting observation. So how would you manage this?

CANDIDATE: It makes more sense to me to represent myself using a radar chart.

Candidate draws following on the whiteboard

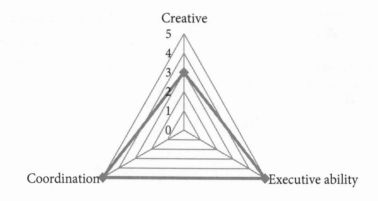

CANDIDATE: I rate myself 5 out of 5 on executive ability and coordination and a three in creativity, and here's why:

	Example
Executive ability	As an Apple product manager, I had to make tough decisions. For example, back in 2009, I told Steve Jobs that we could not ship a fingerprint scanner on the

	iPhone. He said I wasn't trying hard enough. I gave him the prototypes to try it himself, and he realized how unreliable the technology was. He backed off.
Coordination	When I worked at HP in 2012, I had to lead an effort that spanned three companies, five organizations, and 1200 people.
Creativity	I am creative at work, especially when coming up with solutions to customer complaints. Back in 2006, when I was a customer service rep, I closed 400 out of 450 customer complaints with a 5 star satisfaction rating. That was the highest score received for anyone at my level.

INTERVIEWER: You make a good point, but I would like you to complete the original exercise using the original diagram, not the radar chart.

CANDIDATE: The best thing to do is to normalize the values on my radar chart and map it to your original diagram. Eyeballing the chart, I believe I would be equally strong on executive and coordination, but a little bit weaker on creativity.

Candidate draws the following:

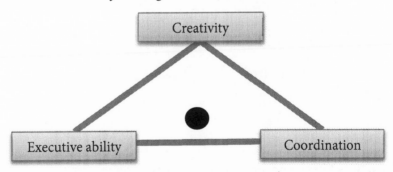

INTERVIEWER: Okay, good.

Comments: This is a question that does not have a correct answer. Instead, it is meant to test your ability to think critically and recognize the flawed question, dissent with the interviewer and propose a constructive alternative.

The candidate started off poorly. He rushed into the question without thinking about the problem. The interviewer jammed him with the response, "so you're not good at creativity and coordination?" From there, the candidate made her position worse by being defensive.

Typically a do-over is awkward and should only be reserved for the most hopeless of situations. In this case, the do-over illustrated how the candidate should have approached the question on the first pass. That is, he should have clarified the objective and question, raised his voice when he detected that the problem setup was amiss, and proposed a better way to solve it.

The candidate also demonstrated his willingness to be flexible by answering the original question setup, by normalizing his selected values, without giving ground.

Chapter 16 Winning the Behavioral Interview

One of my colleagues called behavioral interviews the free throw of interview questions. It's an apt description. On the one hand, behavioral interviews seem like a breeze relative to these difficult case questions. On the other hand, just like basketball, outcomes can be won or lost by a few missed free throws. In other words, don't take the behavioral section of the interview too lightly.

Behavioral interviews are questions about your past experiences. They typically begin with either "Tell me a time…" or "Give me an example…"

Common Behavioral Interview Questions at the PM Interview

Tell me a time when you…

- developed customer and product requirements
- convinced engineering to build a particular feature
- made a tradeoff between two technical alternatives
- created the product roadmap, vision and strategy
- led a team
- dealt with a difficult team member
- executed a plan that grew top line results
- took initiative when not asked to do so
- made an important decision under time pressure
- analyzed a large data set
- gained consensus
- adjusted your project plan to accommodate unforeseen issues
- juggled multiple projects at once
- managed the complete product lifecycle

The behavioral questions can range from leadership to influencing others to end-to-end product management experience.

Why Behavioral Interviews Are Becoming More Popular

Savvy hiring managers are incorporating more behavioral interview questions into PM interviews. These hiring managers have found that behavioral interviews are the best predictors of employee success. For instance, if they asked you, "Tell me a time when you convinced engineering to build a particular feature," the hiring manager would know that if you were presented with a similar situation in the future, you would perform similarly, if not better.

What Interviewers Are Looking For

For an ideal response, interviewers are looking for two things: credibility and likability.

For credibility, they're assessing whether you have the competence to do the job. Here are some factors they want to see in your response:

- **Owner vs. participant**. In today's cross-functional organizations, many interview candidates claimed they led a big project or delivered big results. However, if you dig a bit deeper, you'll find the candidate played a marginal role. Or the candidate may have participated in portions of the project, not the entire thing. To uncover the truth, savvy interviewers will ask follow-up questions including who was involved, what you personally did, and how you did it. It may feel uncomfortable to receive 20 questions on a particular experience, but I have found that it is your benefit to play along. It will more quickly answer the doubts that percolate in the interviewer's mind.
- **Good vs. great achievement**. Interview candidates are clever. They realize that including numbers into their resumes and

interview responses sound more impressive. But even savvier interviewers will want to determine why it was considered a great vs. good achievement. And they want to know whether the results were largely due to your impact, or if those results would have occurred even without your involvement. Expect the interviewer ask follow up questions on baseline metrics such as "How much growth did you see last year?" or "What was the projected increase had you decided not to invest in a new feature?"

We've established your talent by choosing and delivering stories that demonstrate your exceptional experiences, skills, and impact. But likability is the other critical piece to the behavioral interview. It's equally important to develop chemistry or rapport with the interviewer.

Interviewers like to advocate candidates that remind them of themselves. They see themselves as talented and entertaining. For interviewers who potentially interview 2-3 candidates a week, nothing can be more tedious than a candidate who can't find a punch line in their responses or talk about their past experiences with the same excitement as watching paint dry.

Not every candidate is a comedian, so I'm not going to press or even encourage you to tell jokes if that doesn't come naturally to you. But you do have to be entertaining and more importantly, earn the listener's full attention.

Your goal is to tell stories in a way that has the listener on the edge of their seat, eager to hear more. To achieve this goal, shift your mindset. Tell your stories like a world-class storyteller. Think of your favorite storyteller. It could be J.K. Rowling, Stephen King, or Steven Spielberg. Thinking through the basics of a satisfying story, there are three key elements:

- **Colorful characters and settings**. People (and places) have names. Characters have motivations, perspectives and emotions. You're at the center of the story, so you'll be the hero. And every hero has a villain. To summarize, don't forget the who, what, why, how and when of what you're describing.
- **Conflict**. Every good story has conflict that needs to be resolved. For instance, Superman can choose to save 100 million people from a flaming meteor in New York City or his girlfriend, Lois Lane, in Des Moines, Iowa. Life is about dilemmas, tradeoffs, and tough decisions. Good conflicts include unreasonable constraints, impossible deadlines, and Earth-shattering consequences.
- **Resolution.** Every story has to be complete. That is, it has to have a satisfying end where the conflict ends. More often than not, the hero wins. But other times, the hero doesn't win. In those circumstances, there are valuable lessons from a loss that needs to be articulated to the listener.

Just because you're discussing a career experience, it doesn't mean you have to recount your career with the same humdrum delivery as a corporate status meeting.

One more tip: every story has a natural progression that covers the beginning, middle, and end. Don't leave the listener wondering: how did it all start? Or make the interviewer think: did you defeat your foe eventually?

How to Approach a Behavioral Interview Question

I do not advocate the STAR (situation, task, action, and result) interviewing method. It's so poorly practiced by interview candidates everywhere that it's become synonymous with a boring, mechanical delivery. I've developed my own framework, which more naturally directs the candidate toward the storytelling principles in the previous section called the DIGS method™. The phrase "Can you dig it?" has two meanings. First, do you understand? Second, are you enjoying the moment? We want interview stories that hiring managers understand and enjoy. Hence, the DIGS method™:

D ramatize the situation

I ndicate the alternatives

G O through what you did

S ummarize your impact

I've refined the DIGS method™ with hundreds of clients. I've always thought that the best way to interview is to pretend that the interview is a casual conversation between two friends. The DIGS method™ will get your there.

What is the DIGS method™?

Dramatize the situation

Imagine this imaginary conversation with a Fortune 500 CEO:

ME: What did you do today?

CEO: I wrote some emails. I went some meetings. And I yelled at some people.

ME: Oh, guess what, I did same exact thing. Emails, meetings, and yelled people. I guess I can do your job.

CEO: No, no, no. You don't get it. When I was writing some emails, I wrote to John Doe, our chief legal counsel. John is trying to fight a $2 billion dollar, anti-trust fine from the European Union. When I was meeting with someone, I was meeting with Jane Doe, CEO of Silicon Valley's hottest tech start-up, to discuss whether they should renew their

10 year advertising partnership worth $10 billion dollars. When I yelled at some people...

ME: Ah, I guess I can't do your job.

The key takeaway: context and details matter. If we reduce our jobs to the core elements, it's just a bunch of emails and meetings. Dramatize the situation and help us understand why your job, project, or product is important.

Indicate the alternatives

This is an optional step, but if you can do it, you'll be a rock star. When I think about behavioral interviews, it's about problem solving. You're solving problems with people, products, processes, etc.

Any good problem solver knows that there's more than one way to solve a problem. So why not describe all the alternative solutions?

Without the alternatives, the listener just might think to him or herself: "What's so special about that? I would have done it the same exact way." Candidates can't settle for being normal. This is the interview. Candidates need to stand out from others. They need to be special.

The use of alternatives uses the same theatrical device as dramatizing the situation: it helps us appreciate why what you did was so important.

In general, you'd want to list three different alternatives. One alternative is not enough. Two is better. Three feels complete. But more than three is not necessary; the listener will feel overwhelmed.

And one more thing, talk about the pros and cons of each of the three approaches. You'll be perceived as thoughtful and analytical, which traits they'll look for in top product managers.

Go through what you did

Drop us off in the front lines of action. Give us the details of what you did. Who did you call? What did you ask them to do? How did they respond? What kind of resistance did you get?

By putting the listener in your shoes, you convince us that you were the front-line owner and driving, not a participant who was lingering in the back-row, several steps removed from the core action and the results.

Summarize the impact

Conclude your story by summarizing the impact. Without a summary, you'll leave the listener with the *So What?* feeling. Show the listener that your actions benefited the business' bottom line.

Clean, crisp numbers make a big impact. Did your project reduce costs by 5% or increase revenue by $100 million? Yes, those numbers are hard to recall. I barely remember what happened last week. And if you don't remember if the revenue increase was $1 or $100 million, estimate the impact, if you must.

If there are instances where you've racked your brain and can't come up with a reasonable (estimated) number, a qualitative statement could work too. It could be a quote from a senior executive who thought you executed the smoothest product launch that he's seen in last five years. It could be a testimonial from a customer who said it was the most innovative feature that your company delivered in 20 years.

Either way, a qualitative statement that validates your impact can be just as good.

Practice Question

1. Tell me a time when you influenced engineering to build a particular feature.

Answer

Tell me a time when you influenced engineering to build a particular feature.

CANDIDATE: In my current role, I'm the monetization product manager for our free email product.

Two weeks ago, Emma, the engineering manager, gave me some bad news, "William, I'm sorry, but we have to remove 160x600 skyscraper ad. My engineering VP told me that the PM team wouldn't mind." I was thinking to myself: "Are you kidding me? Wouldn't mind? This ad was only the 3rd most valuable ad placement on the entire site. It delivered $75 million in revenue per year. Who did Emma think was paying her salary?"

After I collected my emotions, I asked Emma, "When are you planning to remove it?" She said, "Two code sprints from now. About 6 weeks."

I told her, "Can you give me three days to pull some data? I'd like to understand the impact of this decision."

After she left, I thought: what could I do? I could have a hissy fit and complain loudly. Or I could immediately escalate to the engineering VP. While I was tempted to go with either or both solutions, I wouldn't get what I want unless I was armed with the facts. Before I figured my plan, I gave my boss a heads-up. He wasn't pleased with engineering's unilateral response, but he agreed with my plan.

I logged into the data warehouse and pulled revenue numbers for the last 12 months. Next I asked to sales team to gauge customer reaction if we no longer made the product available. Lastly, I reached out to the VP Engineering's Chief of Staff to better understand why we wanted to remove the ad.

After I collected the data, I set up a meeting with Emma, my boss, and the VP of Engineering. The VP of Engineering reiterated his decision to remove the skyscraper ad. He maintained what I had heard earlier: the skyscraper ads were the reason why the email product's engagement and market share was down.

I asked him, "Why do you think the ads impact engagement?"

He said, "They distract the user."

I replied, "Are there times when you don't find the ads distracting?"

He said, "Yes, when it's relevant to the content. Let's say I'm reading an email about meeting with friends, and the ads suggest things new restaurants and bars.

So I summarized, "So, you don't have a problem with ads. What you're really concerned about is the quality of the ads."

I recommended that rather than remove the ads completely, we should revisit our ad policy and make sure that we're serving relevant ads. We can tighten up our ad editorial processes so that low quality ads aren't mindlessly approved by the system.

He was shocked when I told him that the ad placement generated $200 million in annual revenue. And he also didn't realize that by pulling the placement, customers would pull advertising budget, primarily because it wasn't worth continuing a relationship with us, given the low ad volume and lack of attractive ad placements, relative to our competitors.

Two months later, we rolled out the new ad policy and approval processes. We minimized many of the low quality teeth whitening, weight loss ads that were known for distracting tactics such as pop-ups, fake navigation, and blinking sections. It required a lot more work on our editorial team and advertisers. Shortly after, we later found that email user engagement did go up by 3%, and most importantly, we preserved $200 million in revenue.

Comments: The candidate presented an engaging story on how he influenced the engineering VP to postpone his decision to remove a critical ad placement. He demonstrated thoughtfulness and maturity. He also indicated quantitative ability and willingness to work with different teams. He also showed creativity in coming up with a unique, final solution that was different from what the engineering VP wanted originally. The first person narrative, use of details, and a complete beginning-to-end story arc distinguishes this example from other candidate's who's delivery may not be as polished.

Acknowledgments

This book wouldn't have been possible without these supporters who provided feedback and advice during the process. For those of you I left out, I apologize for the unintentional omission.

Adam Phillabaum	Nabeel Aasim
Ankur Kalra	Nikhil Singhal
Annie Lee	Omar Garcia
Brenton Webster	Omar Garcia
Bruce Jaffe	Paul Travis
Christine Ying	Rodrigo Vaca
David Diskin	Sabra Goldick
Don Alvarez	Sandi Lin
Edward Baik	Scott Shrum
Ingrid Stabb	Shane Menchions
Jamie Hui	Thomas Clavel
Jim Carson	Tim Tow
Kintan Brahmbhatt	Vele Samak
Llew Roberts	Zachary Cohn
Moazzam Ahmed	

Additional Readings

Product Design

The Design of Everyday Things by Don Norman

In this best-selling book, the author introduces and explains key design concepts such as affordances, feedback, and consistency, through everyday products.

About Face 3: The Essentials of Interaction Design by Alan Cooper

One of the most comprehensive books I've encountered on design interaction design process and principles.

Process Improvement

The Goal by Eliyahu Goldratt

This highly readable book explains the keys to improving any process or operation.

Strategy

What is Strategy? by Michael E. Porter

This treasured classic is a 21-page discussion and definition of strategy by the father of modern day strategy, Michael Porter.

Creativity

Thinkertoys: A Handbook of Creative-Thinking Techniques by Michael Michalko

Michalko offers an endless number of creative thinking techniques to help you become more innovative.

Google

***In The Plex: How Google Thinks, Works, and Shapes Our Lives* by Steven Levy**

Written by renowned Newsweek writer, Steven Levy, *In the Plex* offers the most detailed glimpse of what Google is really like, based on hundreds of first-hand interviews with current and former Google employees.

Amazon

***The Everything Store: Jeff Bezos and the Age of Amazon* by Brad Stone**

Brad Stone provides surprising insight on what's known to be one of the most successful, yet secretive companies in the tech industry.

29141795R00121

Made in the USA
Lexington, KY
14 January 2014